Maths Trails
Excel at Problem Solving

Graeme Brown Jennifer Piggott

CAMBRIDGE
UNIVERSITY PRESS

CAMBRIDGE UNIVERSITY PRESS
Cambridge, New York, Melbourne, Madrid, Cape Town, Singapore, São Paulo, Delhi

Cambridge University Press
The Edinburgh Building, Cambridge CB2 8RU, UK

www.cambridge.org
Information on this title: www.cambridge.org/9780521700436

First published 2008

Printed in the United Kingdom at the University Press, Cambridge

A catalogue record for this publication is available from the British Library

ISBN 978-0-521-70043-6 paperback

ACKNOWLEDGEMENTS

NRICH is part of the family of activities in the Millennium Mathematics
Project (www.mmp.maths.org) at the University of Cambridge.

Cover design by Tim Elcock.

The authors thank Steve Hewson, for many valuable suggestions and for
assistance with the spreadsheet files.

Contents

Introduction

The emphasis of this book is on the art and techniques associated with the act of mathematical problem solving. The book contains 23 problems which benefit in some way from having a spreadsheet available, either as a ready-made environment to explore or as a tool for helping the solver create a model to use in their search for a solution. Not all problems require a spreadsheet in order to be solved. The emphasis is, rather, on how a spreadsheet could potentially help. A spreadsheet can help to reveal a pattern which it might otherwise be difficult to spot or labour-intensive to produce. In these situations the spreadsheet does not explain why the pattern is what it is (the bit of mathematics we are really interested in) – that is the task of the problem solver. However, when part of the task is the production of a spreadsheet, it is necessary for the solver to understand and represent the mathematics within the problem. This is at the heart of the experience for the learner.

This book is aimed principally at teachers of pupils between the ages of 11 and 16. Each problem is accompanied by guidance that includes information on prerequisite knowledge, lesson outlines and solution notes. Additional teaching resources, supporting spreadsheets and pupil reference sheets are included on the CD-ROM. Links are also given to complementary material on the NRICH website (www.nrich.maths.org). Resources on the NRICH website can be located either by using the date of publication in the text or by typing the name of the resource into the search box on the site.

The book is written to promote three main ideas:

- problem solving;
- using spreadsheets to help in posing or solving problems;
- learning spreadsheet skills that can make the solution of problems less labour-intensive.

The problems in this trail have been chosen because they lend themselves to being tackled with the aid of a spreadsheet – although none of them demands the use of a spreadsheet. You could therefore use this book for the problems and ignore the spreadsheet aspect of the trail altogether but clearly this would miss the point! The real challenge is for the problem solver to be able to identify the benefits for themselves. We suggest interspersing problems in this book with others that are less likely to benefit from the use of a spreadsheet and encouraging pupils to identify opportunities for the use of spreadsheets for themselves.

One issue you may have to deal with is that of pupil expectation. Many pupils expect to have to use the equipment as soon as they walk into a computer room. One way to overcome the tail of Information and Communications Technology (ICT) wagging the mathematical dog is to introduce problems in advance of the main lesson and invite pupils to think about potential routes to a solution. Remember that elegant solutions can be obtained in ways other than through the use of a spreadsheet. Having access to a computer does not mean that you have to use it! Able pupils may often find a very elegant algebraic solution and the principal aim should be to solve the problem not to use the spreadsheet. The NRICH website often includes solutions to problems that have not made use of a spreadsheet, so it is worth taking a look.

Problem solving and mathematical thinking

The purpose of this maths trail is to help give some meaning to problem solving with a particular focus on using spreadsheets. This book forms part of a series of titles which includes *Generalising*, *Working Systematically* and *Visualising*. Each book looks at particular skills that can be useful in the problem-solving process. While this collection of books promotes particular problem-solving skills, working through them is not on its own a measure of an expert problem solver.

This book is about encouraging pupils to 'be mathematical' in the sense that they:

- engage in problem-solving activities;
- think about and communicate their ideas;
- create and identify mathematical problems within given contexts.

Being mathematical and doing mathematics in this sense involves some mathematical content knowledge, but mathematics is more than learning facts and practising skills and we need to support learners in 'being mathematical' in this deeper sense. We need to offer them the opportunity to be problem solvers who pose and explore their own problems. This book offers some guidance and structure upon which to focus if we are to support pupils' problem solving effectively.

What is problem solving?

When we are presented with a mathematical problem, it is only a problem if we do not immediately know how to solve it. This means that something that is a problem to one person may not be a problem to another. The process of problem solving is like a journey from a state of not knowing what to do towards a destination which we hope will be a solution. The key is to have some strategies at our fingertips that will help us to identify a possible route through to a solution. Our mathematical journey is often full of twists and turns, where we revisit ideas or need to step back and look for alternatives. Often a mistake or dead-end gives vital clues to the mathematics of the problem and is therefore crucial in any solution process.

To help us have a sense of direction when we are problem solving and decide what might be a good strategy to try next, it can be useful to have a model. There are many problem-solving models but the one below is a good starting point. Although the steps are written in sequence, the diagram emphasises the reality that problem solving can be a messy process which often involves revisiting places on the journey from problem posing to problem solving.

Spreadsheets can play an important role in many of the stages of the problem-solving process.

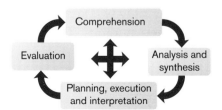

Comprehension

This stage is about making sense of the problem by using strategies such as retelling, identifying relevant information and creating mental images. Pupils can be helped at this stage by being encouraged to re-read the problem several times, or to investigate the context by trying things out, and to record what they understand the problem to be about (for example, by drawing a picture or making notes).

Environments that encourage exploration, such as those created within a spreadsheet program, can motivate pupils to 'get stuck in' – to want to discover what is going on. Similarly, the idea of using spreadsheets as a support for solving the problem can give pupils just enough of a nudge in a useful direction to get them going. Evidence suggests that the use of ICT can be a motivation in itself.

Analysis and synthesis

This stage is about 'homing in' on what the problem is asking solvers to investigate.

- Can they represent the situation mathematically?
- What is it that they are trying to find?
- What do they think the answer might be (conjecturing and hypothesising)?
- What might they need to find out before they can get started?

Central to this stage is identifying what is unknown and what needs finding. Here pupils might think about what information they might include in a spreadsheet – giving a focus for their search. If pupils are exploring a ready-made environment the immediate feedback from any exploration can not only clarify their ideas but encourage them to pose problems of their own.

Planning, execution and interpretation

Once pupils have understood what the problem is about and have established what needs finding, the next stage is about planning and executing a pathway to the solution. It is within this process that you might encourage pupils to think about whether they have seen something similar before and what strategies they adopted then. This will help them to identify appropriate methods and tools. Particular knowledge and skills gaps that need addressing may become evident at this stage.

As pupils think about techniques that would be useful and how a spreadsheet might help, they need to be planning an approach to solving the problem. There is a complex interplay between considering how a problem might be solved and building up a model. Careful thought needs to be given to the representation of variables and controlling change. There is likely to be continual movement between planning and execution, with refinement and review forming an integral part of the solution process. Pupils may need additional encouragement to write down their findings when they are using a computer.

During the execution phase, pupils might identify further related problems they wish to investigate. They will need to consider how they will keep track of what they have done and how they will communicate their findings. This will lead on to interpreting results and drawing conclusions.

Evaluation

Pupils can learn as much from reflecting on and evaluating what they have done as they can from the process of solving the problem itself. During this phase pupils should be expected to reflect on the effectiveness of their approach as well as those of others, to justify their conclusions and assess their own learning. Evaluation may also lead to thinking about other questions that could now be investigated.

When pupils have used a spreadsheet they should be encouraged to discuss how the use of ICT helped them, whether they used the technology efficiently and how the technology opened up, or constrained, possibilities. In lesson plenaries, you may wish to introduce spreadsheet techniques that might have made a solution more efficient. These can be followed up in later lessons.

Using the model

The use of a problem-solving model has a number of benefits in the classroom.

- It is a structure that can help pupils frame their problem solving and keep track of where they are in the process.
- It gives us a language which helps us to talk to pupils about what they are doing. For example:
  - 'Can you tell me what you think the problem is about?'
  - 'What are you trying to find?'
  - 'Have you seen anything like this before and what did you do then?'
  - 'Could you have solved this in a different way?'
- It offers a framework which can help structure lessons so that you can plan what pupils might do at various stages.

We think it is very important to draw the attention of your pupils to the model during their work on each task. Many of the activities involve engagement with all aspects of the problem-solving 'cycle' but certain problems lend themselves to focusing on particular aspects that can be highlighted and made a focus for the lesson.

What is mathematical thinking?

Within the problem-solving framework, there are many other mathematical skills which pupils need to have at their fingertips. These skills involve more than numeric, geometric and algebraic manipulation. They include strategies such as:

- modelling;
- visualising;
- working systematically;
- generalising.

These elements of mathematical thinking are needed to engage in the problem-solving process. The problems presented in this book encourage a number of these aspects of mathematical thinking. For example, many of the problems require pupils to understand a ready-made spreadsheet model or create a model of their own.

The 'excel at problem solving' trail

The trail structure is shown over the page and runs from left to right. The problems are in a suggested order with more difficult problems (related to mathematical content knowledge, the level of the problem solving needed or ICT skills) further along the trail.

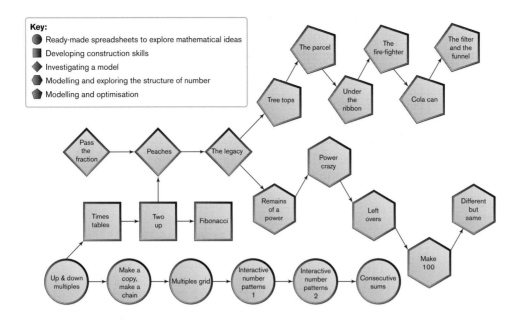

Key:
- ● Ready-made spreadsheets to explore mathematical ideas
- ■ Developing construction skills
- ◆ Investigating a model
- ⬟ Modelling and exploring the structure of number
- ⬠ Modelling and optimisation

Why use this trail?

The problems in the trail support problem posing as well as the problem-solving process. The trail attempts to offer a range of contexts which require spreadsheets to be used in different ways.

- Firstly, the spreadsheet can act as an environment where the pupil is asked to investigate what is happening and then try to explain it. A simple example of this can be found in 'Interactive number patterns 1'. Here, the environment needs to be explored and the underpinning mathematics explained. These environments may be used as a stimulus for class discussion or for individuals or small groups to act upon.

- Secondly, the spreadsheet may act as a labour-saving device, enabling the user to generate a large amount of information out of which it is possible to spot patterns. For example, in 'Make 100' the spreadsheet does not explain the pattern but helps the solver to generate enough examples for a pattern to emerge. The challenge is to explain the pattern.

- Thirdly, the spreadsheet can be used to achieve rapid repeated calculation. This allows the solver to focus on the context, such as searching for an optimal solution, rather than the calculation itself. There are two types of problem of this general kind.
  - In the first type the model is already created for the user, as, for example, in 'Remains of a power'. In this case pupils move towards an understanding of what the model is doing. We describe this process of examining the structure and making sense of the formulae used as 'deconstruction'.
  - In the second type pupils create a model for themselves, as in, for example, 'Tree tops'. Here they unpick the underlying mathematics in order to understand what is needed and construct a model for themselves.

In engaging with the problems in this book pupils might:

- investigate a pre-programmed model to identify patterns and relationships and its underpinning rules;
- investigate the consequences of altering the values of variables in a model;
- design and construct models of their own;
- evaluate models and share ideas.

How to use the trail

This trail is an organised set of curriculum resources, including teacher notes and hints for pupils, designed to develop purposeful use of a spreadsheet. The trail contains 23 problems and a guide to the Excel techniques used throughout the book. The trail has three main pathways:

- ready-made spreadsheets to explore mathematical ideas;
- mathematical tasks that can be used to build confidence with using spreadsheets;
- problems which explore mathematical structure and optimisation.

We have divided this last type of resource into three main categories. Firstly, there are problems where learners are invited to explore a ready-made model and secondly, there are problems where the model gives opportunities to explore the structure of number. Finally, we have included problems that involve using a model to aid optimisation. We suggest that the problems offered of the first type are the most accessible and therefore might be attempted before moving on to exploring the structure of number and/or optimisation.

Sometimes we place an emphasis on deconstruction of existing spreadsheets and at other times the emphasis is on pupils constructing their own spreadsheet models. In any activity where we suggest the construction of a spreadsheet by pupils you may feel it is more appropriate for pupils to work on understanding the structure of a pre-prepared spreadsheet. We therefore have included ready-made spreadsheets for all the problems.

You might wish to use the trail as a 'course' for pupils over a short or long period of time, with them working as a whole class, in small groups or individually. The trail indicates an ordering of the materials to support each pupil's developing skills over time. However, it is also possible to dip in and out of the materials at appropriate points in a scheme of work. The timings indicated in the teacher notes for each unit are indicative as the intention is to encourage extension and pupil investigation beyond what is made explicit. The trail is not intended to be a strait jacket.

The problems offer opportunities for pupils of a wide age and ability range, and do not imply a particular view of classroom organisation. However, there is an underlying message concerning classroom practice and the learning of mathematics as a collaborative experience, valuing the journey through a problem rather than just the answer. While it is not necessary for pupils to work in groups, there is an expectation that pupils will be given opportunities to talk about their mathematical experiences *en route* as well as at the 'conclusion' of their investigations.

Questions to consider when using spreadsheets

The following questions may serve as a useful focus for reflection on the use of spreadsheets.

- What aspect of mathematics is the work addressing? Is it doing so successfully?
- What prerequisite skills are needed before starting the task (mathematics and ICT)?
- Is any specific vocabulary needed in order to be able to talk effectively about the activity, the model or the outcomes?
- How is the spreadsheet work supporting the mathematics being covered?
- Is using the spreadsheet enabling you to do things you would not have been able to do better (or as well) another way?

Ideas for managing sessions

There are no step-by-step rules that will always lead to a solution in any of the problems we have used in this book. The aim is to encourage pupils to share ideas and different approaches and learn to value those differences while identifying elegant and efficient solutions whenever appropriate. After working on this trail, pupils should feel able to recognise where the use of a spreadsheet might be helpful and feel empowered to use the ICT skills they have learnt appropriately and more effectively when problem solving in the future.

The lesson notes included in this book are intended purely as a guide. As indicated in what follows, there are as many approaches to teaching as there are pupils in a class! All we can do is offer some ideas without any intention of being prescriptive.

Working with the whole class

The following might be a typical whole-class approach to a problem.

Introduce the problem

Building on the introductory activity, introduce the problem and, where it is helpful, start to model an approach or share your thoughts on what mathematics underpins a situation. Then ask the pupils to work entirely on their own for five minutes – giving them time to experiment and to familiarise themselves with the context. At this point it is worth emphasising that pupils are not expected to be working neatly towards a solution, either in terms of what they might do with an existing spreadsheet or in terms of what a spreadsheet they are going to create for themselves might look like. They are simply finding out what the problem might be about. After a short time you will stop them and ask them to work with a partner in order to share what they have discovered or thought about. The aim of the time spent working in small groups and pairs is to share initial ideas which can then be discussed as a whole class. This part of the lesson corresponds to the 'comprehension' phase of the problem-solving process.

Sharing and moving on

Stopping pupils after a short period of time to share findings and ideas of what the problem is about offers opportunities to 'get started' for those who have not found a way into the problem and the chance to refine and develop ideas as a community. It is not enough to 'know how to do it' but to leave room for new ideas and questions to be discussed. This is about valuing the journey, including the cul-de-sacs we may encounter or the different routes we may take. During this time pupils are beginning to identify potentially promising approaches to tackling the problem.

Planning, execution and interpretation

So far we have encouraged our pupils to:

Think – Pair – Share

After these early discussions pupils need further time to investigate the problems and consider possible routes to their solutions, create spreadsheet models of their own and/or consider further problems that might arise. Sharing and iteration of discussions will help to give all a sense of owning the mathematics and ensure that, as far as possible, as many different approaches to the problem are considered, not simply 'the answer'.

Evaluation

During this last phase pupils discuss their findings, convincing themselves, and their classmates, that any findings they have or conjectures that they wish to put forward are reasonable. Time considering different solutions and their 'efficiency' or 'accessibility' are invaluable in opening up the mathematics and helping pupils value different approaches. Discussing the value that the use of spreadsheets has brought to the problem is an essential element of any lesson. Then, of course, it is worth considering all the other problems or ideas that the context has stimulated pupils to consider, and the process can start again!

Working with individual pupils

Trails can also be a useful tool for teachers to use with individual pupils who need the challenge of problem-solving activities that have the potential to incorporate the use of ICT. Pupils who quickly grasp the mechanical aspects of mathematics and/or ICT but find it difficult to work on open-ended tasks can be encouraged to tackle some of the problems in the trail. The sense of direction and purpose in the trail, when shared with the pupil(s), can give them the opportunity to build up a repertoire of approaches to such problems, particularly in emphasising where there are opportunities to use spreadsheets, and give them more confidence when confronted with similar activities in the future.

Working with groups

Groups of pupils can often find their own way into problems simply by being given the context and being asked to:

- identify what the question is about;
- consider strategies for solution;
- plan what they are going to do;
- execute their plans.

One important aim might be to encourage pupils to communicate their findings to others in the class or their teacher, describing the problems they had as well as how they chose their methods and executed their solutions. This communication does not have to take the form of written output but could be verbal or in the form of a poster or presentation.

Finally encourage the group to answer evaluative questions such as:

- Could we have done this more efficiently?
- What have we learnt that is new?
- Have we met anything like this before? Were we able to make connections?
- What additional questions did we come up with and answer while we were working on the problem?
- Are there some questions still to be answered?
- How did the spreadsheet help?

Many further examples of problems are available on the NRICH website (www.nrich.maths.org) if you wish to extend any of the work in a particular area of mathematics or simply to reinforce ideas and skills. Happy trailing!

Assessment

Prerequisite knowledge

Three aspects to pupils' prerequisite knowledge need to be considered.

Firstly, we need to consider pupils' abilities to tackle problem-solving situations independently. This trail emphasises the importance of applying problem-solving and mathematical thinking skills and, while it continues to employ and develop those skills, complementing the work in other books in this series, it does not assume any particular proficiency in or familiarity with problem solving. As the main purpose of the trail is to support, develop and extend these skills, it means that, as a teacher, the amount of scaffolding and support you will be offering will vary considerably according to pupils' prior experiences of problem solving and their individual needs.

Secondly, each problem depends upon knowledge of particular aspects of mathematical curriculum content.

Lastly, a problem may assume familiarity with a particular spreadsheet skill.

Assessment for learning

The notes and other documentation for each problem aim to support formative and summative assessment opportunities. Outline solutions to problems are included to give some guidelines on expected outcomes. Edited pupil solutions can be found to many of the problems on the NRICH website at www.nrich.maths.org. The advantage of looking at solutions on the website is that they can give you an idea of the variety you can expect from your pupils.

In some cases, it might be best not to highlight the content objectives at the beginning of the lesson as doing this could close down possibilities for pupils to think independently. We therefore suggest that the lesson objectives shared with the pupils should not 'reveal' obvious routes to a solution.

Listening and questioning are important tools in the process of formative assessment. To support this:

- all problems have suggested prompts for teachers and mentors to use;
- pupils are encouraged to hypothesise and share ideas with fellow pupils, arguing their case – these are ideal opportunities to listen;
- whole-group discussions during the lesson can be used to reveal pupils' understanding, misconceptions or lack of awareness of, or confidence in, the necessary mathematical knowledge;
- peer assessment can often shed valuable light on the understanding of the assessor as well as the assessed;
- reviewing and reflecting on the lesson outcomes with the pupils can help the teacher make judgements and also be used by pupils as an opportunity for self or peer assessment.

As highlighted earlier, much of the work and learning is about the journey through each problem. It is not necessary for pupils to have well-rounded, written solutions for sound assessment judgements to be made. While feedback through marking is sometimes appropriate, oral and continuous feedback throughout the problem-solving process is just as valuable.

'To be effective feedback should cause thinking to take place'
Assessment for learning in everyday lessons (DfES, 2004)

Assessing learning over the whole trail

In any problem there is the potential for four main outcomes:

- the introduction, development or consolidation of an aspect of mathematics;
- application and practice of problem-solving skills;
- practice and extension of capability with spreadsheets;
- application of mathematical understanding and technology to the solution of a problem.

As a result of having ICT and mathematical outcomes attached to any task there is a need to find the balance which does justice to them both. Associated with this balance is the way in which ICT is integrated into the teaching and learning. Do ICT skills need to be learnt separately, in advance of their application, or can they be successfully integrated into the mathematics lesson without losing the focus on mathematics? It is worth reiterating that all the activities in the book place the emphasis firmly on the mathematics. Some additional time may be needed to support the ICT needs of your pupils, or help your pupils support each other in securing the particular techniques they might need when creating a spreadsheet or modifying an existing spreadsheet. Often this 'additional' time (what we call the 'ICT overhead') should not be very large in any single unit. If pupils use spreadsheets regularly, they will build up expertise and any new technique will only be a small step on from where they already are. In addition, ICT lends itself to peer support. Our experience in the classroom indicates that some pupils already have the skills needed or can pick them up very quickly and help others in the class. It is not necessary for the teacher to have to teach every child every new technique individually.

Resources

The resources for every problem include a range of spreadsheets in a single Microsoft Excel workbook file, along with supporting problem and resource sheets. The content of each Excel file reflects the nature of the activity and, as a result, their content varies. Each element of the resource is referred to within the book's text. The nature of the content of each spreadsheet is very dependent on the unit it supports.

- Units where pupils will be using the spreadsheet as an interactive environment may contain more than one sheet, each with slightly different versions of the environment. These pre-configured conversions enable the teacher and pupils to focus on and develop particular aspects of the problem.
- Units where pupils are expected to produce spreadsheet models of their own will have Excel workbooks with sheets that contain examples of what to expect. These sheets can be used for demonstration purposes or for teacher reference.
- Units where pupils may be expected to explore an existing spreadsheet and amend it in the course of their work will contain Excel workbooks with partially completed sheets that can be used for demonstrating particular points, as well as completed examples of possible solutions.
- Where a new Excel technique might be used the Excel workbook contains a tutorial sheet.
- Solutions are often contained within the example spreadsheet and where this is the case they are referred to in the text.

Excel workbooks normally contain more than one spreadsheet – accessible via the tabs at the bottom of each sheet. Tabs have been colour-coded to help you find your way around:

- blue for sheets which might form an integral part of the lesson;
- green for supplementary sheets;
- red for example solution sheets;
- yellow for techniques.

The spreadsheet techniques are also included in the final section, 'Some Excel techniques explained'.

Excel techniques and use of the CD-ROM material

The use of ICT normally involves a tension between the learning of skills and the application of those skills. Many pupils are taught ICT skills in isolation. This book promotes a view that the ICT is there to support and enhance the mathematics. The need to develop and practise skills should arise naturally from the needs of a problem. The skills that might be required are part of a single learning experience for the pupil. Through engaging in the tasks in this trail pupils will:

- learn about spreadsheets through problem solving;
- use spreadsheets to support the problem-solving process.

Some skills are usually assumed. Pupils must be able to:

- input formulae;
- copy and paste;
- save different versions of the same sheet.

Other important techniques are described within the units where they occur, with technical instructions in the section 'Some Excel techniques explained' at the end of the book. In summary these are:

- **Using a graph.** Optimisation problems (for example 'The filter and the funnel' or 'Cola can') can be managed without a graph by examining the values in cells, but adding the graph offers a view of how the function behaves generally and can enrich our understanding of the problem and its solution.

- **Relative and absolute references.** This option enables a single cell value to control many other cells without losing the ability to swiftly replicate formulae using **Fill down** and similar techniques. In 'Make 100' and 'Different but same' this choice between relative and absolute references enables a complete table of results to be produced from a single formula.

- **Conditional formatting** can be enormously useful because it makes conspicuous the values that are of particular interest. These values could be located by simple cell-by-cell inspection, but colour change via conditional formatting not only picks these values out but often draws attention to pattern as, for example, in 'Power crazy'.

Finally there are two functions in Excel that are well worth knowing about from a problem-solving point of view. The **MOD** function produces the remainder and is used, for example, in 'Remains of a power'. The **INT** function separates the integer and decimal parts of a number and is used to powerful effect to isolate the digits within a value.

Computer screen specifications vary. The display size for any spreadsheet can be adjusted using **Zoom** on the **View** menu.

Some further reading

Burton, L. (1984) *Thinking Things Through*. Oxford: Basil Blackwell.
Mason, J. with Burton, L. and Stacey, K. (1982) *Thinking Mathematically*. Wokingham: Addison-Wesley.
Piggott, J. (2005) 'An investigation into the nature of mathematical enrichment: a case study of implementation'. Ph.D. dissertation, Institute of Education, London.
Polya, G. (1945) *How to Solve It*. London: Penguin.

Up & down multiples

Ready-made spreadsheets to explore mathematical ideas

Prerequisite knowledge
- Number bonds
- Experience of thinking systematically

Why do this unit?

This unit offers opportunities to make and test hypotheses concerning effective strategies for winning the 'Up & down game'.

Time

One lesson

Resources

CD-ROM: spreadsheet
NRICH website (optional):
www.nrich.maths.org, November 2007, 'Up & down multiples'

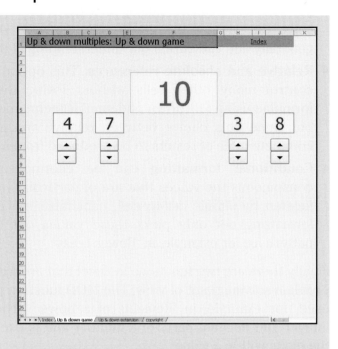

Introducing the unit

Use the 'Up & down game' on the spreadsheet.

Click the spinner buttons to show how the total changes. An up arrow adds the number above it to the total in the blue box and a down arrow subtracts. When demonstrating the spreadsheet make sure that the total at some point becomes a multiple of 10 so that pupils see the change in colour that this causes.

Next, click on one of the numbers above the spinner buttons (not on the buttons themselves). Use the keyboard to type in a different value and press **Enter**. Click the up and down arrows a few times to see the total change by this new amount.

Check that pupils understand how the sheet works by asking them how to get the total to zero. Check their suggestions using the spreadsheet.

The rules of the game

The 'Up & down game' is played between two people or two teams. The objective is for a team to make the total a multiple of 10 after two clicks of their spinner buttons. When a positive multiple of 10 is reached the game continues

without a return to zero. The first side to achieve a multiple of 10 three times wins the game.

Each team chooses a single-digit number (excluding 5) which is typed above one of the spinner buttons on their side of the screen. Each team then chooses one more spinner button number, but this time for their opponents. That number is typed above the second button on their opponents' side.

On a turn a team must always make two clicks somewhere on their spinner buttons. For example, they might go up twice on the same button, or might make one click on each of their buttons. However, their two clicks cannot be up and down on the same button because that is equivalent to not taking a turn.

A game might start like this:

Team A with spinner button numbers 4 and 7 is playing against team B with spinner button numbers 3 and 8. The total is zero.

Team A starts and chooses 'up 4, up 4' so the total is now 8.

Team B then chooses 'up 8, down 3' and the total becomes 13.

Team A then chooses 'up 4, up 7' making the total 24.

Team B scores with 'up 3, up 3' (total 30). The game continues from 30.

Play a game

Play the game once or twice with the whole group.

Main part of the unit

You could continue the game as a whole-class activity, but by playing in pairs or small groups pupils can identify and justify strategies to share later in the lesson and in the plenary. Encourage the class to stay focused by exploring strategic questions.

- What numbers make good combinations? [Some pairs of spinner button numbers create options that are more useful than others. For example, having both numbers even or both odd only allows the total to be changed by an even amount.]
- Why is 5 not allowed? [After an opponent scores, two clicks on 5 make an immediate return score.]
- How would you defend against particular moves? [Work out the complete set of moves that are possible. Any two spinner button

numbers will give a limited set of possibilities. It is only the units (last) digit that matters – a total of 21 and 51 present the same challenge.]

- Extend the game and your strategies by scoring on multiples of other numbers (see 'Up & down extension' on the spreadsheet). What is the same and what is different?

It may be useful to stop the class from time to time to share ideas and challenge strategies. This will help pupils move on in their thinking and prepare them to offer feedback in the plenary.

Plenary

Pupils with strategies to share can use and explain them. Others can consider and challenge the justifications offered for the choice of strategies and talk about how they would play to defend themselves (defensive strategies) in response.

Playing the game once or twice as teams at the end of the lesson enables pupils to see whether they have improved their performance and are thinking more strategically.

Solution notes

Some number pairs allow more flexibility. For example, 4 and 7 allow changes to the total of 3, 8, 11 and 14 so a score is possible from a previous total ending in any digit but 5.

Make a copy, make a chain

Ready-made spreadsheets to explore mathematical ideas

Prerequisite knowledge
- Multiplication facts

Why do this unit?

The 'Make a copy' activity (resource sheet) is a good way to maintain and extend pupil familiarity with tables. 'Make a chain' (problem sheet) offers an opportunity for pupils to pose their own challenges.

Time

One lesson

Resources

CD-ROM: spreadsheet, problem sheet, resource sheet
NRICH website (optional): www.nrich.maths.org, November 2007, 'Make a copy'; March 2007, 'Factor-multiple chains'

Make a copy

Resource sheet

A

	6	15	9	12
	12	30	18	24
	18	45	27	36
	4	10	6	8

B

	18	12	27	6
	48	32	72	16
	30	20	45	10
	36	24	54	12

C

	28	12	32	36
	63	27	72	81
	56	24	64	72
	49	21	56	63

D

	10		20	
		27		18
	16		32	
		18		12

E

		18		
	8		20	
		27		72
		25		

Maths Trails: Excel at Problem Solving | Problem and resource sheets   © Cambridge University Press 2008

Introducing the unit

Show the class the sheet 'Grid A' and ask:

- How are the numbers in the grid produced by the blue numbers at the edge? [by multiplication]
- How do the spinner buttons change the blue values? [increase or decrease]
- Can you choose particular blue numbers so that the grid on the left is the same as the grid on the right?

Allow plenty of time for pupils to share their reasoning.

Grids B to E are similar puzzles. Later puzzles need solving using less given information.

The resource sheet 'Make a copy' contains a version of the same puzzles and one blank grid for pupils to make a challenge of their own.

Main part of the unit

Display the sheet 'Factor multiple chains'.

A complete line like $3 \leftrightarrow 6 \leftrightarrow 30 \leftrightarrow 90$ is referred to as a 'chain' because adjacent numbers are related factor to multiple. The values in each blue box can range from 2 to 100. Check that pupils understand how the sheet works by creating other chains.

Encourage use of the terms 'factor' and 'multiple' by making statements like '30 is a multiple of 6' and inviting pupils to offer the other. [6 is a factor of 30]

Ask pupils to work in pairs on the challenges posed on the problem sheet 'Make a chain', pausing for discussion at intervals.

Invite pupils to pose and pursue similar challenges of their own.

Plenary

Discuss the reasoning used for the challenges on the problem sheet and for pupils' own challenges.

Solution notes

Make a copy

A	2	5	3	4
3	6	15	9	12
6	12	30	18	24
9	18	45	27	36
2	4	10	6	8

B	6	4	9	2
3	18	12	27	6
8	48	32	72	16
5	30	20	45	10
6	36	24	54	12

C	7	3	8	9
4	28	12	32	36
9	63	27	72	81
8	56	24	64	72
7	49	21	56	63

D	2	3	4	2
5	10		20	
9		27		18
8	16		32	
6		18		12

E	2	3	5	8
6		18		
4	8		20	
9		27		72
5			25	

Make a chain

$2 \leftrightarrow 4 \leftrightarrow 8 \leftrightarrow 16$ is the smallest complete chain.

The chain $5 \leftrightarrow 25 \leftrightarrow 50 \leftrightarrow 100$ produces the largest possible number in the last three positions but $12 \leftrightarrow 24 \leftrightarrow 48 \leftrightarrow 96$ contains the largest number possible in the first position.

26 cannot be in a chain. If it were possible, the latest it could appear would be position two with either 2 or 13 in position one but position four is limited to a number up to 100 and so cannot offer a value to make a chain. Also prime numbers must occupy position one in any chain in which they appear.

88 is the maximum difference between adjacent numbers in a chain. [$2 \leftrightarrow 4 \leftrightarrow 8 \leftrightarrow 96$]

For the greatest possible range $2 \leftrightarrow 4 \leftrightarrow 8 \leftrightarrow 96$ looks promising [94] but $5 \leftrightarrow 25 \leftrightarrow 50 \leftrightarrow 100$ is greater still [95].

The minimum range is 14 produced by $2 \leftrightarrow 4 \leftrightarrow 8 \leftrightarrow 16$.

Multiples grid

Ready-made spreadsheets to explore mathematical ideas

Prerequisite knowledge
- Multiplication facts

Why do this unit?
This unit reinforces the concepts of multiples and common multiples and leads to an exploration of the underpinning structure.

Time
One lesson

Resources
Squared paper
CD-ROM: spreadsheet, resource sheets 1–6
NRICH website (optional):
www.nrich.maths.org, March 2007, 'Multiples grid'

Multiples grid

Resource sheet 1

Window on the grid

2	3	4
12	13	14
22	23	24
1

34	35	36
44	45	46
54	55	56
2

24	25	26
34	35	36
44	45	46
3

31	32	33
41	42	43
51	52	53
4

24	25	26
34	35	36
44	45	46
5

14	15	16
24	25	26
34	35	36
6

5	6	7
15	16	17
25	26	27
7

34	35	36
44	45	46
54	55	56
8

56	57	58
66	67	68
76	77	78
9

66	67	68
76	77	78
86	87	88
10

| Maths Trails: Excel at Problem Solving | Problem and resource sheets   © Cambridge University Press 2008

Introducing the unit

Ask pupils to work in pairs at a computer for five minutes on the sheet 'Number grid multiples'. At the end of that time ask pupils to offer their observations to the whole group. Pupils may observe that multiples of the chosen numbers are coloured pink or blue, and common multiples are coloured maroon.

- Can any selected number in the grid be made pink, blue, maroon or uncoloured? [Yes, except for 1, which is always uncoloured.]

Main part of the unit

Window on the grid

Work together on the first two grids from 'Window on the grid' on resource sheet 1.

- What settings could result in these two grids? [Pink is 3, blue is 7 or 14; pink is 4, blue is 5.]

- Can you justify that? Check the solution using the sheet. [Notice how sometimes there is more than one right answer.]

It is important to allow plenty of time for discussion, drawing attention to efficient methods of covering all cases. For example, if the 16 on the grid is blue then the blue setting must be 2, 4, 8 or 16 (factors of 16).

When the group is confident and ready to move on, pupils can try the remaining 'windows' on the resource sheet and perhaps generate examples of their own with which to challenge each other.

Printing wallpaper

Use the image from 'Printing wallpaper, Pattern 1' on resource sheet 2. Discuss the structure of the pattern. 'Pattern 1 without numbers' (resource sheet 3) may help pupils identify patterns more easily.

- What do you see? [For example, part of the pattern goes blue–pink–blue vertically, or the maroon steps down evenly, or …]
- What could the setting numbers have been? [pink 6, blue 4]

This pattern with coloured blocks can be made using a basic unit as a stamp, and stamping repeats of that unit, side by side, until the whole grid space is covered.

- What would the stamp unit look like? [any rectangle of width two and height six]

Discuss the structure of 'Pattern 2' (resource sheets 4 and 5) similarly. [The settings are pink 2, blue 5, with a single whole row as the repeating unit.]

Invite pupils, working in pairs, to find the basic stamp unit for other settings and explain any relationships they notice between the basic stamp and the setting numbers used.

Ask each pair of pupils to choose one grid pattern to print, superimposing their stamp unit and adding their conjectures and reasoning. Use these printouts to make a group display.

Plenary

Invite pupils to look at the patterns on display and to talk about any common features they have noticed.

Solution notes

Window on the grid

The table below shows the pink and blue settings which produce each window on resource sheet 1.

Window	Pink	Blue
1	3	7 or 14
2	4	5
3	3	9
4	6	7, 14, 21 or 42
	7, 14, 21 or 42	6
5	2	7
6	3	4
7	4, 8 or 16	9 or 27
8	6	3 or 9
9	3	8
10	8	11

Printing wallpaper

If one of the setting choices is 2, for all choices of the other setting (n, $n < 10$), the stamps are all 2 wide and n deep giving an area of $2n$ square units with the exception of 5×5. The rule breaks down here because multiples of 5 are vertical and therefore do not cut across the vertical lines of the multiples of 2.

By considering the slope of the diagonals of multiples of other n it is also possible to justify the 'heights' of the stamps.

For $3 \times n$ ($n < 7$) and $4 \times n$ ($n < 7$), similar justifications for the arrangement of stamps can be made.

If the two numbers have common factors this affects the ability to make a rectangular stamp. So 3×9 and 4×8 work.

It is possible to look at other grid widths to examine what stamps are made.

Interactive number patterns I

Ready-made spreadsheets to explore mathematical ideas

Prerequisite knowledge

- Use of symbols to represent unknown or varying values
- Use of algebraic expressions to represent relationships

Why do this unit?

This interactive environment allows pupils to explore number sequences and their algebraic representation. 'Interactive number patterns 2' extends the work here to quadratics.

Time

One lesson

Resources

CD-ROM: spreadsheet
NRICH website (optional):
www.nrich.maths.org, September 2007,
'Interactive number patterns 1'

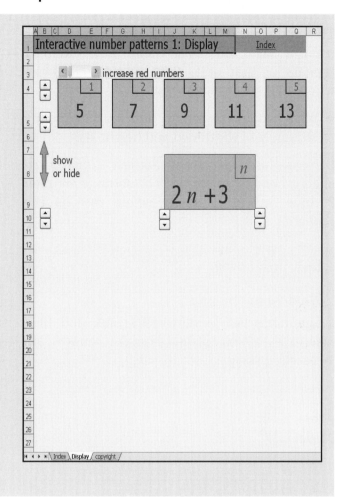

Introducing the unit

Open the spreadsheet and familiarise the group with it. Check that pupils understand:

- the slider at the top changes the red numbers;
- the spinner buttons on the edge of the formula box change the numbers in the formula;
- the three spinner buttons on the left of the screen hide or show parts of the display.

The purpose of this part of the activity is to familiarise pupils with substituting values into given formulae and to predict the sequence of blue numbers.

Set the formula to $2n+3$ and set the red numbers to read 1 to 5.

- Why is the first blue number 5? [Substituting $n = 1$ in the formula gives $2 \times 1 + 3 = 5$.]
- Why are the other blue numbers 7, 9, 11 and

13? [similar substitutions of 2, 3, 4 and 5 into the formula]

Hide the blue numbers and invite pupils to suggest changes to the formula. Ask pupils to predict the hidden blue values and record their answers. Repeat this process with different formulae, keeping the red values 1 to 5. Have pupils propose formulae, predict the blue values and then check. Extend the activity by changing the red values using the slider but keep the calculations easily within the ability of the group so that their focus remains on the algebra not the calculation.

Continue this activity but hide the red values instead of the blue.

Pupils will be solving equations mentally, though they probably will not think of it like that, and now is a good opportunity to invite pupils to share their methods.

Make sure that these two processes of substituting and solving to find unknown or hidden values are well practised before moving to the main activity.

Main part of the unit

The purpose in this part of the activity is for pupils to arrive at a method for determining the formula which has been used to generate the terms within a displayed sequence. There are a number of ways that the spreadsheet can help. Here are two approaches.

Open investigation

Ask pupils to work in pairs to devise a method that can successfully predict the hidden formula. The method is then shared with the group and the presenters are asked to explain why their method works. If a justification is not possible for the presenters, other pupils may be asked if they can see and explain why that method works. Invite the group to explain how the offered methods compare. Ask pupils to say which method they like best and why.

Whole group

Set the red numbers to start at 1 and set the formula box to $2n$.

- Do you notice any pattern in the blue numbers? [They go up by 2.]

Discuss how the $2n$ makes this happen and then look at $3n$, $4n$ and $5n$ similarly. Some pupils might use phrases like '$2n$ is the algebra for the two times table'.

Return the formula box to $2n$, drawing attention to the blue values ascending by 2, and change the formula to $2n+1$. Point out that the blue numbers still increase by 2 as before but with every value getting a 'bonus 1' from the $+1$ in the formula. Extend this to cover any constant between -10 and 10.

If time allows, pupils can work in pairs to test each other's understanding by taking turns to hide various elements of the spreadsheet for the partner to complete, before checking.

Plenary

Working with the whole class, ask pupils to 'look away' while one pupil changes the formula and then hides it so that the red and blue values are all that show.

Model to the group how you would determine the formula. For example: 'First I notice the step size – the increase between blue values – that tells me the value of the number of n in the formula. Next I think what it would be if it was that many n and nothing else (like a times table). I compare that with the actual blue number and that tells me how much bonus or loss every term is getting.'

Invite pupils to 'look away' with you each time. Offer your model initially but move towards pupils offering their own descriptions of the process.

Ensure that a good range of red values is used.

Interactive number patterns 2

Ready-made spreadsheets to explore mathematical ideas

Prerequisite knowledge
- Substitution into formulae
- Linear equations
- Quadratic expressions

Why do this unit?

The interactive environment allows pupils to explore quadratic sequences and their algebraic representation. This unit is suitable for pupils for whom 'Interactive number patterns 1' is very straightforward.

Time

Two lessons

Resources

CD-ROM: spreadsheet, resource sheet
NRICH website (optional):
www.nrich.maths.org
September 2007, 'Interactive number patterns 2'

Interactive number patterns 2

Resource sheet

Introducing the unit

Open 'Patterns (simple)' on the spreadsheet. Ensure that pupils understand:

- the slider at the top changes the red numbers;
- the spinner buttons on the bottom edge of the formula box change the numbers in the formula;
- the spinner buttons on the left of the screen hide or show parts of the display.

Set the formula to $n^2 + 7n + 4$ and the red numbers to read 1 to 5. Check with the group that substituting n as 1 into the expression gives 12, and continue with $n = 2$ through to 5 to produce 22, 34, 48 and 64.

Hide the blue numbers, ask for changes to the formula, and invite pupils to predict the hidden blue values. Include examples where the red n values range up to 20.

Continue this activity but hide the red values instead of the blue. Once the red values are hidden, set the formula back to $n^2 + 7n + 4$ and use the slider at the top to change the first blue number to 202.

- What red value produces the blue of 202? [11]
- How did you work that out? [Pupils may say 'trial and improvement'.]

Show the red values and reset the formula to $n^2 - 10n + 10$. Drag the slider to the extreme left to show blue values of 1, −6, −11, −14, −15.

- When n is 1 the formula gives 1. For what other n value will the formula also give 1? [9]
- Are there any other n values that produce 1? [No, after 9 the function continues ascending indefinitely.]
- Which n value produces 21? [11]
- Is there a second value which also produces 21? [Not within the limits of this spreadsheet, but $n = -1$ makes $n^2 - 10n + 10 = 21$.]

Make sure that pupils understand fully the process of substituting to find unknown or hidden values before moving to the main activity.

Main part of the unit

The aim of this part of the activity is for pupils to arrive at a method for determining the formula used to generate the terms within a sequence. It is common for pupils to use a method based on the difference between values, and then the difference between those difference values. It is less common for pupils to grasp the validity of this method. This activity is designed to improve pupil understanding of the 'difference method'.

Set the formula to $n^2 + 3n + 8$ and move to 'Patterns with differences' on the spreadsheet. (Note that changing the quadratic expression and/or the red values on one sheet automatically updates the other.) Many values are displayed on this sheet and it is important that pupils are given time to understand each part.

There are three rows below the formula box. These display the values of the quadratic, linear and constant terms from the quadratic formula respectively. Change the terms in the formula box to help pupils grasp what each row shows. Verify that the three values added together produce the blue function values in the boxes at the top of the screen. Draw attention to the two rows of differences above the formula box and verify that the data showing is the correct difference for the blue function values. Change the red values using the slider and have pupils verify the new values displayed within the sheet.

- What changes when we alter the red values and what stays the same? [The first difference changes; the second difference remains unaltered.]

- Why? [The constant term contributes nothing to the first difference; the linear term contributes to the first difference but not the second; the coefficient (multiple) of the quadratic term is the only coefficient influencing the second difference.]

Return to 'Patterns (simple)'. Change the formula and ask pupils to write what the other sheet would show if they could see it. (There is a template for this on the resource sheet which enables pupils to record their solutions prior to discussion.)

Return to 'Patterns with differences' to compare pupil answers with the display and discuss.

Repeat this exercise as a group or ask pupils to work in pairs, with one of them altering the formula for the other to explain, until they are familiar with the role of differences.

Use 'Patterns with differences' and set the formula to $2n^2$ with no linear or constant term. Discuss the effect of the 2. Change the 2 to 3, 4 and then 5, discussing the effect until the group is confident that for a quadratic sequence the second difference will always be constant at double the coefficient of the quadratic term. Ask them to explain why this is true. Allow plenty of time for discussion as this is a central objective for this activity.

Ask pupils to work in groups to determine rules for finding a formula for any given sequence.

Plenary

Pupils discuss and evaluate some of their methods, leading to a whole-group challenge to determine hidden formulae for given sequences.

Consecutive sums

Ready-made spreadsheets to explore mathematical ideas

Prerequisite knowledge
- Simplification of algebraic expressions

Why do this unit?

The sum of consecutive integers occurs frequently in mathematics. This activity uses an interactive spreadsheet to assist visualisation, leading to a key formula, and tests conjectures about sums of consecutive numbers.

Time

Two lessons

Resources

CD-ROM: spreadsheet, problem sheets 1 and 2
NRICH website (optional):
www.nrich.maths.org, May 2004, 'Sequences and series'; December 2001, 'Proof sorter – sum of an AP'; May 1997, 'Consecutive sums'

Consecutive sums

Problem sheet 1

Adding consecutive numbers

First do it the long way. Add up 1 + 2 + 3 + 4 + 5. What's the answer?

Now see the pattern another way.

The sequence can be written a second time in reverse order.
1 + 2 + 3 + 4 + 5
5 + 4 + 3 + 2 + 1

Notice that each number in the lower line makes a sum of 6 with the number directly above it.

Why do all these individual pairs have the same total?

In all, there are 5 of these pairs, all of which make 6, so the total of all the numbers in both lines must be 5 lots of 6 (that's 30).

Both lines have the same total so they must be 15 each (30 divided by 2).
So now we know that the numbers 1 to 5 have a sum of 15.

What about the sum of the numbers 1 to 10?
Write them down in line and again in a second line but backwards.
What will each number in the lower line make with the number directly above it this time?
How many pairs will there be?
So what is the total of all the numbers together in both lines?
And then you'll know the total in each line.
You have found the answer to 1 + 2 + ... + 10 but without having to add them all!

Try finding the sum of 1 to 20 using this method.

What is the sum of the numbers 1 to 50? to 100? to 1000?

Could you write a formula explaining how to sum 1 to n?

Can you see how to use this method to add 10 + 11 + ... + 20?

| Maths Trails: Excel at Problem Solving | Problem and resource sheets   © Cambridge University Press 2008

Introducing the unit

The introductory activity aims to give pupils an efficient means of adding a long sequence of consecutive numbers.

Open 'Quick adding' on the spreadsheet and explain to pupils that this sheet shows the calculation $1 + 2 + 3 + \ldots + n$. Tell pupils that they are going to find a quick way of doing the calculation, even when the numbers are large and there are lots of them.

Use the spinner buttons by the top table to show the results for $n = 6$, 7, 8, 9 and 10. Adding the consecutive numbers 1 to 6 gives a total of 21, 1 to 7 gives 28 and so on.

- Can you see a connection between the last number in the sequence and the total (sum) we arrive at? [Each time the total increases by the value of the last number – 6 makes 21, 7 makes 28, 8 makes 36, 9 makes 45 and 10 makes 55.]

- What do you notice about 21, 28, 36, 45 and 55? [They are triangle numbers.]

Set n to 6 and point out the arrangement of numbers in the sheet. 1 to 6 is above 6 to 1. Draw attention to the sum of each column, 7, as the upper number is added to the number below it.

- Why is this total the same all the way along? [Values ascend in the upper line and descend in the lower line by the same amount.]

- What is the sum of each pair? [One more than the largest number, $n + 1$.] How many columns are there? [n]

- So what is the total of both rows all together? [$n(n + 1)$]

- And what must the total for one line be? [$\frac{1}{2}n(n + 1)$]

Ask pupils to check this for enough specific n values until they have a strong understanding of the result and can justify it and use it.

We have looked at consecutive numbers which start at 1. What happens if we do not start at 1? Problem sheet 1 may be helpful at this stage. Choose a few examples to clarify what is being discussed and invite pupils to suggest methods for finding the sum. Some pupils may suggest a method similar to the method when starting at 1 (reverse and add in pairs, multiply and halve). Other pupils may suggest a subtraction method (the sum of 16 to 100 is equal to the sum of 1 to 100 minus the sum 1 to 15).

Main part of the unit

Show the problem 'Consecutive sums' on problem sheet 2. Explain that the class is going to work in pairs to find sums using consecutive numbers that need not start from 1.

As pupils work in groups on the problem some questions to stimulate discussions might include:

- Do you notice which numbers can be formed from the sum of two consecutive numbers? [All the odd numbers – because with two consecutive numbers one must be odd and one even.]
- Why can't you make an even number from two consecutive numbers? [As above.]
- Can you think of a quick way of finding the two consecutive numbers? [Roughly half the odd number $\frac{1}{2}(n+1)$.]
- What numbers can be represented by three consecutive numbers?
- What about four or five consecutive numbers? [Related to multiples.]

- Is there a method for producing more using the answers you already have? [There are many methods but an example might be: 'If I have $15 = 4 + 5 + 6$ then I can go up from 15 in steps of 3 by adding one to each number like this: $18 = 5 + 6 + 7$' – this justifies the multiples suggested in the question above.]
- Can you predict what consecutive sums are possible given any number? [Yes, by looking at its factors.]

Investigate sums that are not possible.

- Are there any numbers you haven't been able to find consecutive sums for? [Pupils may offer quite a few but through discussion, reduce this to powers of 2.]

Plenary

'Sums' and 'Sums zoom 20%' on the spreadsheet automatically calculate sums of consecutive numbers and are available to support discussions in the plenary.

There will be lots to share from the main activity but you may wish to focus on one idea that has been noted but not justified. For example, prove that pure powers of 2 can never be made as the sum of consecutive numbers.

Follow this by asking pupils to justify the conclusion to each other and to produce a proof in their own words on paper.

Solution notes

Plenary

Visually: This particular image happens to have nine strips but it is offered as the general case, so the number of strips (number of consecutive numbers) could be odd or even.

If the number of strips is odd, the longest and shortest strips will either both be even or both odd. This means their sum (the width of the rectangle) must be even. In either case the rectangle in the image has its height odd and its width even.

If instead the number of strips is even, the longest and shortest strips will be odd and even (or even and odd) respectively – so their sum must be odd. In this case the rectangle in the image would have its height even and its width odd.

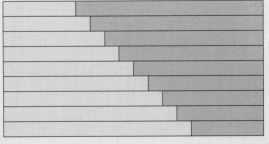

However, if we need to arrange a power of 2 into a rectangle, both dimensions must be even, and this cannot be done with an odd or an even number of strips, so cannot be done at all.

Algebraically: $\frac{1}{2}n(n+1)$ always contains an odd factor because either n or $n+1$ must be odd, and the other one even. The even factor can be divided by the 2 but the overall result must always contain an odd factor, and pure powers of 2 will only have even factors, so they will never match the sum for a set of consecutive numbers.

Times tables

Developing construction skills

Prerequisite knowledge
- Spreadsheets as tables
- How to create or copy formulae is not required as this is one of the anticipated outcomes of the activity

Why do this unit?

This activity focuses on number properties and precedence of numerical operations. It also develops basic spreadsheet skills. Pupils with more advanced skills can be encouraged to use absolute as well as relative referencing to create two-way tables, such as multiplication tables.

Time

Up to one lesson

Resources

CD-ROM: spreadsheet, problem sheet

Times tables

Problem sheet

Can you find at least four ways of creating the four times table using the numbers in the one and two times tables and the four operations?

How many different ways of making the four times table like this do you think there are? Justify your answer.

Which of the four operations did you use to create the four times table? Can you create the four times table using subtraction or multiplication?

When you are ready, investigate the different ways you can make the six times table. Did anything surprise you?

Can you make the six times table by multiplying, adding or subtracting columns?

Can you explain any findings?

On a new spreadsheet, create the two and three times tables as efficiently as you can.

Why do you think you were efficient?

How often did you have to write in values or formulae?

Extension

It is possible to create a full set of multiplication tables starting with the integers at the top of the rows and in the first column and by entering just one formula.

Use the spreadsheet 'Gridsheet' to start.

You might also find the idea of **absolute references** useful!

| Maths Trails: Excel at Problem Solving | Problem and resource sheets   © Cambridge University Press 2008

Introducing the unit

Demonstrate how a spreadsheet can be used in the production of the one and two times table (see 'Sheet 1' on the spreadsheet).

Ask the class to re-create the one, two and then the three times tables in the same way.

Pupils who move on quickly can be encouraged to think of other ways in which they could produce the three and four times table without multiplying by 3 and 4 respectively and by only using the entries in columns A and B plus the four operations (+, −, ÷, ×) and brackets. For example, to create the three times table they could add entries in column A to themselves three times or add column A entries to column B entries. The aim is for pupils to share their ideas with the rest of the class in the main part of the activity.

Encourage groups to produce tables in different ways. Use row 3 to write the formulae they have used, for reference (see 'Sheet 2').

Main part of the unit

Once the class is making good progress and is demonstrating an ability to create and copy formulae it is time to move on.

Share ideas on how they might create the four times table using only columns A and B. (It might be useful to use groups who have already thought about this to guide the discussions.)

- How many different ways do you think you can make the four times table using columns A and B? Five ways? Ten? [as many as you like]
- Can you describe some of your methods? Let's test them and see.

Ask the group to work in pairs to create the four times (and then the six times) table in as many ways as they can just using columns A, B and C on 'Sheet 2'. Ask them to write their formulae on the board plus any surprises that they discover. The problem sheet is available to support this part of the unit.

One idea that might surprise pupils is the fact that the two times table multiplied by the three times table does not give the six times table. However, it is possible to correct the formula so that it does give the six times table, for example by dividing by column A (the one times table).

- Why does that work?

You might like to introduce some rules and a scoring system for creating the formulae. For example, rules might be:

- You cannot use an operation more than twice.
- You are not allowed to add and then subtract the same number or multiply and then divide by the same number because these are inverse operations.

A scoring system might be:

- Addition and/or subtraction   1 point
- Multiplication   2 points
- Division   3 points
- Brackets   4 points

- The use of all four operations in one formula   5 points extra

In this way you are encouraging the group to be adventurous.

Extension

If some of the pupils have a sound grasp of the process, challenge them to produce a multiplication grid up to 20 using as few formulae as possible starting with the numbers 1–20 as in 'Gridsheet' on the spreadsheet.

For more confident pupils 'Sheet 4' gives an example which utilises absolute references and requires only one formula.

Plenary

Discuss some of the more imaginative formulae and surprising outcomes. Why are they all equivalent? Some examples might lend themselves to simple algebraic manipulation to explain the equivalence.

Solution notes

See sheets 1, 2 and 3 on the spreadsheet for some ideas.

The six times table cannot be produced by multiplying the two times table by the three times table because this would mean that you have included the multiplier twice.

For example, $5 \times 6 = 5 \times 2 \times 3$. Multiplying the two entries in the two and three times table would give you $5 \times 2 \times 5 \times 3$ – you are out by a factor of 5. This can be remedied by dividing by 5 (the value in column A).

Two up

Developing construction skills

Prerequisite knowledge
- Symbolic notation to represent a mathematical idea
- Enter and change data on a spreadsheet

Why do this unit?

This activity offers pupils opportunities to pose their own problems and to employ algebra to aid justification. The use of the spreadsheet and the feedback it offers enables pupils to focus on patterns and relationships without being overwhelmed by the calculations.

Time

One lesson

Resources

CD-ROM: spreadsheet, problem sheet

Two up

Problem sheet

What questions would you like to ask? Spend some time exploring the spreadsheet and changing things before you resort to using some of the ideas below.

Remember to make a note of your conjectures and write down explanations of what you find so that you can share your ideas and reasoning with other people later.

Here are some things you might think about if you cannot think of a question of your own:

- What things could you change?
  - the start number
  - the number of rows in column 1
  - the multiplication table
- What questions could you ask about changing the start number?
  - Can I see a pattern to the end number for different start numbers?
  - What happens when I change the multiplication table?
  - How can I make the end number the same if I keep the start number the same?
- What questions could you ask about changing the end number?
  - How does the end number depend on the start number?
  - How does the end number depend on the times table I use?
  - Can I work out a rule for the end number that takes account of different start numbers and tables?
- Can you work out the end number if someone tells you the start number, the table and the number of rows? Is there a rule that always works?
- Can you work out the start number for any multiplication table, number of rows and end number?
- Are some end numbers impossible under certain conditions?

Introducing the unit

Model how to create the run of 'counting numbers' on a spreadsheet and how to create multiples of 2 using the counting numbers (see 'Two up (T)' on the spreadsheet (red tab)).

Use your own spreadsheet or 'Two up' on the spreadsheet (blue tab) and change the value of cell A2 several times. Ask the group to account for some of the new values appearing in the other cells.

- What will the final number in the first column be if I change the 1 in cell A2 to a 5, a 10, a 101? [24, 29, 120]
- What would be the first number if the final number was ...?
- What will be the final number in the second column if I change the 1 in A2 to 4, 31, 1000? [46, 100, 2038]

Ask questions about how the spreadsheet was constructed.

- How else could I make the two times table in column B using the numbers from column A? [e.g. add each number to itself – demonstrate the equivalence on the spreadsheet in column C.]
- Will it have the same effect on the rest of the spreadsheet if I change the number in cell A2?
- What about other ways?

Ask pupils to work in pairs to create their own copy of 'Two up'. You may wish to make the original sheet available for the pupils to refer to. Both pupils in a pair should be able to demonstrate that they can confidently create this sheet.

Pairs should then test each other's understanding by asking questions about the final number in the second column for different starting numbers (and vice versa).

Main part of the unit

- What number would I have to put in cell A2 to make the final number in the second column 162? [62 – an interesting result as both numbers end with the same two digits]
- Are there other start numbers for which the last number is 100 plus the start number? [See solution notes.]

Ask the pupils to investigate this and to seek a generalisation of their results.

The problem sheet contains further conjectures and ideas to pursue. Encourage pupils to pose their own problems by giving them a few minutes to explore and think about questions of their own before letting them see the suggestions on the problem sheet.

- What other questions do you want to ask?
- What things can you change? [start number, number of rows in column 1, which multiplication table to use]
- What questions could you ask about changing the start number?

- Can you find a rule for describing the end number whatever the start number and the table that is used?

Ask pupils how they would like to share their findings in the plenary. They could:

- note each conjecture they decide to focus on;
- record their findings and arguments related to the conjecture.

Focus on things that surprised them and what information they needed to keep on the way.

Plenary

Select one or two 'surprising' findings to share with the class. Pupils do not have to be able to describe generalisations algebraically but identifying two or more different explanations pupils have for the same generalisation during the lesson and sharing these will encourage pupils to think that it is possible to have more than one correct solution in mathematics.

Solution notes

The only start value which produces an end value greater by one hundred is 62. $2(x+19) = 100 + x$ leads to $x = 62$.

However, changing the column length from 20 and looking for $x \geqslant 100 + x$ gives $2(x+n-1) = 100 + x$ where x is the start number and n is the numbers added on.

This leads to $n = (100 - x + 2)/2$ or $x = 100 - 2n + 2$.

Changing the tables from 2 to 3 times yields:
$3(x+n-1) = 100 + x$
$2x = 100 - 3n + 3$
$x = (100 - 3n + 3)/2$ (for this to work n must be odd)

For example, if $n = 21$, $x = 20$ and the end number is 120.

Fibonacci

Developing construction skills

Prerequisite knowledge

- Understanding the idea of a sequence, and that a sequence can be generated using different methods. For example, 2, 4, 6, 8, ... can be created by starting with 2 and forming each new term by adding 2 to the previous term, or by multiplying the term number n by 2 ($2n$)
- Create formulae in a spreadsheet

Why do this unit?

This activity encourages pupils to become familiar with a well-known sequence and explore its properties. Pupils make hypotheses and then either justify or disprove them. This activity is also a useful context in which to reinforce the understanding involved in key technical skills: editing a formula, **Copy**, **Paste** and **Fill**.

Time

One or two lessons

Resources

A3 sheets of paper and pens
CD-ROM: spreadsheet, problem sheet
NRICH website (optional):
www.nrich.maths.org, October 2000, '1 step 2 step'; May 2005, 'Sheep talk'. These problems

result in the Fibonacci sequence and make useful complements to this activity.

Fibonacci

Problem sheet

Fibonacci sequences

- What happens when you add the same Fibonacci sequence to itself? Do you get a Fibonacci sequence? Can you explain what you discover?
- What happens when you add two different Fibonacci sequences (with different start values)? Do you get a Fibonacci sequence? Explain your findings.
- What happens when you add a multiple of one Fibonacci sequence to a multiple of another?
- Are your explanations convincing? Will you be able to convince the rest of the class?
- Can you extend your findings to more than two Fibonacci sequences?
- Do you find the same things when you subtract, multiply or divide terms in two Fibonacci sequences?

Extension

- Can you build a sequence from two consecutive terms that are somewhere in the middle of the sequence? For example, can you find other numbers in the sequence containing ..., 33, 53, ...?
- What happens if you are given two non-consecutive terms such as 31, ☐, ☐, 131? Is there a way to generate the sequence? For example,

| Maths Trails: Excel at Problem Solving | Problem and resource sheets   © Cambridge University Press 2008

Introducing the unit

The Fibonacci number sequence (named by the French mathematician Edouard Lucas after the 13th century Italian mathematician) starts: 1, 1, 2, 3, ... Similar sequences that have a different initial pair (1, 3 or 2, 5 for example) are called Lucas numbers. Other sequences of numbers formed using slightly different rules have particular names (e.g. Pell numbers). In this activity, the process of adding terms to produce a next term we will call the 'Fibonacci process' and the resulting sequences 'Fibonacci-like' sequences.

Ask pupils to imagine the numbers 2, 4, 6, 8, ...

- What is the next number in the sequence? [10] And the next? [12] And the next? [14]

- How about the 10th term? [20] How do you know? [There are several valid answers including 2×10.]

- Now imagine another sequence 1, 2, 4, 7, ... Can you describe what is happening here? [The step size is increasing by one.]

- Can you tell me the next three terms in this sequence? [11, 16 and 22]

Main part of the unit

Ask the group to think about 0, 1, 1, 2, 3, 5, ...

- Can you describe how each term is formed and give the next three terms? [Add two consecutive terms to obtain the next term; 8, 13, 21]

Explain that this is called the Fibonacci sequence – it is a sequence where each term is formed by adding the two previous terms.

Demonstrate how to create a Fibonacci sequence. Start from an empty spreadsheet or use the blue tabbed sheets on the spreadsheet provided. Inspect cells and ask pupils what each formula calculates until the sheet's structure is understood.

Draw pupils' attention to how the first two values control all that follows. Change the values to demonstrate this – here the 'Fibonacci' sheet could be used. Discuss the structure through questions such as:

● What initial values make the 5th term 13? [2 and 3]

Once a general feel for a Fibonacci sequence has been established ask:

● What happens if we add two of these sequences together? (see 'Adding-T' on the spreadsheet)

Encourage pupils to suggest hypotheses which they can begin to test for themselves.

● How can you check the sum is a Fibonacci sequence? [The sum itself could be generated by creating the sequence from its first two terms.]

Ask pupils to investigate other properties of Fibonacci-like sequences, using the problem sheet for guidance.

Encourage pupils to write their conjectures on A3 conjecture sheets and post them up on the wall to write on as they test, explain and extend their ideas. These will form the focus of the plenary.

As the pupils work on the tasks encourage them to record their findings and explanations on their conjecture sheets, emphasising the importance of being able to produce a convincing argument. Encourage them to ask questions of their own if they notice something of interest.

Pupils who are struggling to produce the spreadsheet for themselves might benefit from being given a pre-prepared spreadsheet (see the blue tab sheets on the spreadsheet).

Note: You might wish to introduce the notation $T_n = T_{n-2} + T_{n-1}$ to those pupils who have a good grasp of algebraic notation.

Extension

● Given two consecutive terms, e.g. 33, 53, subtracting 33 from 53 gives the preceding term (20, 33, 53). Repeat this process until sufficient terms are found.

● Given 31, x, y, 131, then $31 + x = y$ and $x + y = 131$. Solve these equations simultaneously.

Plenary

Encourage pupils to share the range of findings they have made.

● Were any of your findings unexpected?

● Which arguments were most convincing?

You can use the pupils' conjecture sheets to support this part of the lesson.

Solution notes

Adding or subtracting two Fibonacci-like sequences or multiplying by a constant results in a Fibonacci-like sequence. Multiplying or dividing sequences does not.

Adding

a	b	$a+b$	$a+2b$	$2a+3b$	...
+	+	+	+	+	+
c	d	$c+d$	$c+2d$	$2c+3d$	...
↓	↓	↓	↓	↓	↓
$a+c$	$b+d$	$a+c+b+d$	$a+c+2b+2d$	...	...

Subtraction and multiplication by a constant work similarly.

Pass the fraction

Modelling and optimisation

Prerequisite knowledge
- Fractions of an amount

Why do this unit?
This activity is designed to support the discussion of problem-solving methods. The problem 'Pass the fraction' can be solved algebraically but a systematic approach quickly narrows down the possibilities. The activity emphasises that there is often value in recording on paper when using ICT.

Time
One lesson

Resources
Counters or plastic coins may be useful
CD-ROM: spreadsheet and resource sheets 1 and 2
NRICH website (optional):
www.nrich.maths.org, March 2002, 'A bowl of fruit'; November 2004, 'Ben's game'; March 2002, 'In the money'

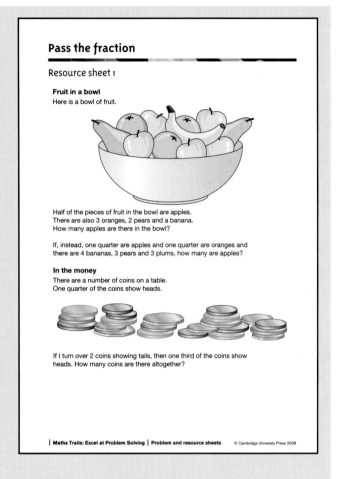

Pass the fraction

Resource sheet 1

Fruit in a bowl
Here is a bowl of fruit.

Half of the pieces of fruit in the bowl are apples.
There are also 3 oranges, 2 pears and a banana.
How many apples are there in the bowl?

If, instead, one quarter are apples and one quarter are oranges and there are 4 bananas, 3 pears and 3 plums, how many are apples?

In the money
There are a number of coins on a table.
One quarter of the coins show heads.

If I turn over 2 coins showing tails, then one third of the coins show heads. How many coins are there altogether?

| Maths Trails: Excel at Problem Solving | Problem and resource sheets   © Cambridge University Press 2008

Introducing the unit

Use the problem 'Fruit in a bowl' on resource sheet 1 as a starting point for discussion.

- What do we know?
- What do we want to know?
- What can we find out?

Now look at the problem 'In the money' on the same resource sheet.

Ask the group to think on their own about how they might tackle this problem. Then ask pupils to discuss their ideas in pairs and get ready to share their ideas with the rest of the group. Where pupils suggest trying some numbers, develop this into a fully systematic approach.

- What do you know about the number of coins on the table? [multiple of 4]

Encourage pupils to try possibilities systematically. Give them some time to work in pairs to find a solution and feed this back to the rest of the group.

Some pupils may wish to use counters or coins to look at the problem practically.

It is possible that a pupil may offer an algebraic approach or one involving direct manipulation of fractions. Each method suggested can be compared with a systematic approach, discussing the merits of each and leaving pupils satisfied that any one of them leads to a solution, although some methods may be more efficient than others.

Main part of the unit

Display the problem 'Pass the fraction' on resource sheet 2.

Tell pupils to spend two minutes working on the problem on their own before sharing their ideas with a partner. After a time stop the group to share ideas and possible approaches.

- What do they know? [Ben must have a multiple of 3 counters, Ravi a multiple of 4…]

If pupils are not offering this insight, turn to the spreadsheet which calculates the number of counters left when pupils input different start values for Ben, Ravi and Emma.

- What is the spreadsheet doing? [Look at each cell to see what it contains.]

Input some possible start values for each person.

- Why are numbers in the grid sometimes decimals? [If the start number is not a multiple of the divisor you will get an answer which is not a whole number.]
- What does this tell us about the numbers of counters each person must have? [They must be multiples of 3, 4 and 5 respectively.]
- Also, what can we say about the total number of counters in use if Ben, Ravi and Emma all have the same at the end? [The total is a multiple of 3.]

The group can now return to the problem. They may still need support as they consider systematic approaches to finding a solution.

- How many different things can you change? [Three – the starting number of counters for each of the children.]

- Can you see how to fix the value of some things while you let one thing go through all its possible values?
- How do you know you have tried all the possibilities?

Explain that the spreadsheet can deal with the calculation but we need to record results in a way that lets us be sure we have all the solutions.

Plenary

Ask pupils, in pairs or groups, to explain what the problem was, what they tried, what their preferred method is and how confident they are that they have every solution (in other words that there is one, and only one, solution here).

The aim now is to give pupils a taste for how a given context can become, by degrees, more general. There is scope here for generalising. Ask pupils to make up similar problems of their own. 'In the money' can be posed with other differences than 'two more', or the fractions themselves might be different. In 'Pass the fraction' the fractions could be different or the number of participants might increase from three to four. It is enough to point out these possibilities, and invite other suggestions from the group, and not neccessary to pursue the new problems at this time.

Solution notes

Fruit in a bowl
6 apples
5 apples and 5 oranges

In the money
A systematic approach might be to test what happens if you start with:

HTTT
HHTTTTTT
HHHTTTTTTTTT
…
Answer: 24 coins.

Pass the fraction
Emma 10, Ravi 8 and Ben 12 counters.

Peaches

Modelling and optimisation

Prerequisite knowledge
- Simple formulae in Excel

Why do this unit?
This activity shows how a spreadsheet can be used to provide results systematically so that patterns can be observed and relationships verified.

Time
One lesson

Resources
CD-ROM: spreadsheet, problem sheet
NRICH website (optional):
www.nrich.maths.org, November 2004,
'Peaches today, peaches tomorrow'

Peaches

Problem sheet

Peaches today, peaches tomorrow

A monkey has some peaches.

He eats half of them plus one more.

The next day, he eats half of the rest plus one more.

On the third day, he again eats half of what he has plus one more.

At the very end of the third day, he finds there is only one peach left.

How many did he have at the beginning?

If on the fourth day, he finds two peaches remain, or three peaches, or four and so on, how many did he have at the beginning?

What patterns do you see? Can you explain them?

Introducing the unit

Show pupils the problem sheet.

Allow a few moments for pupils to think about the problem and to share their ideas with a partner. Move into whole-group discussion and focus on trial and improvement. For example:

- How many peaches are left at the end of day 3 if there were 30 peaches to start with? [2]

Go through the calculation together in readiness for looking at the spreadsheet.

Main part of the unit

Go to 'Peaches 1' on the spreadsheet.

The sheet is set for 30 peaches. Discuss the contents of each cell and how that connects with the discussions so far.

Change the 30 in cell A3 to 20 and verify the values that appear. Point out that 20 could not be the solution because it does not result in a whole-number answer.

- Why do decimal values appear in the sheet? [Dividing numbers by 2 several times will frequently lead to a decimal answer.]

Ask the group to work in pairs using 'Peaches 1', and changing the value in A3, first to find the number of peaches that leave 1 at the end of day 3, and then to find the start numbers that leave 2, 3 or any whole number of peaches.

After a short time show the 'Peaches 2' sheet and ask the pupils why this sheet is an improvement. [We can see which numbers work, keep track of what we have tried, and notice patterns.]

Show the group how 'Peaches 2' has been created from 'Peaches 1' using **Fill down**.

Ask pupils to continue with the task. As they work, the following prompts may be useful:

- Why do negative values appear in the sheet? [Trying to take more than is there will generate a negative result.]

- Why is it good to start at 1? [We need to work systematically.]
- Which numbers help us answer the question 'How many peaches did the monkey start with?' [Whole-number values in the 'Peaches left after day 3' column.]
- Can you explain why whole numbers appear in steps of eight?

Extension

Working backwards can be a powerful problem-solving strategy. This problem offers an excellent opportunity to demonstrate that skill to some pupils using the 'Peaches backwards' sheet.

- Can you explain how this sheet solves the problem? [The 'half plus one' means that the other (uneaten) half lost one which needs adding back to get a true half. That is then doubled to return to the whole before halving. That process happens three times to get us back to the starting number of peaches.]

Plenary

Allow plenty of time for the main activity to be discussed and understood. Draw out key points that you have noticed while observing pupils working, including how a spreadsheet displays calculation results but does not explain any patterns or account for them.

Create a shared table of results, for example:

Number of peaches left	Peaches at start
1	22
2	30
3	38
4	46
5	...
...	...

- The pattern of start peaches goes up in steps of eight with 14 added in each case [$8n + 14$]. Why?

Solution notes

The 'Peaches backwards' sheet on the spreadsheet gives the first few solutions.

Whole numbers of peaches appear at regular intervals. A group of 8 peaches is halved three times until only one remains, so the remaining number at the end of the third day increases by one for every eight extra peaches at the start. For n peaches at the end of day 3 there must be $8n + 14$ peaches at the start. If the process took place over four days you would expect the step size to be 16 ($2^4 = 16$).

Explaining the 14 by working backwards. Imagine you finish with n peaches. This means that on the penultimate day there would have been $2(n + 1) = 2n + 2$ peaches. And on the day before: $2(2n + 2 + 1) = 4n + 6$. And on the day before that: $2(4n + 6 + 1) = 8n + 14$.

The legacy

Modelling and optimisation

Prerequisite knowledge
- Percentages and interest
- Formulae in a spreadsheet

Why do this unit?
The aim is to investigate the strengths and limitations of different models of investment. The lesson notes are based on pupils exploring, comparing and evaluating the models that are given.

Time
Two lessons

Resources
CD-ROM: spreadsheet, problem sheet, resource sheets 1–5
NRICH website (optional):
www.nrich.maths.org, November 2007, 'The legacy'

The legacy

Problem sheet

A school has been left £1 000 000 in the will of an ex-pupil. The constraints on how the money should be invested and used are:

- The money should have a lifetime of approximately 50 years.
- The school must benefit in some way (spend part of the investment) every year.

You have been asked to evaluate models of investment and expenditure based on any balance being invested at different rates of interest and possibly considering different inflation rates.

What model would you choose to ensure the best return for the school over a period of 50 years (or longer if you wish)?

Introducing the unit

Turn to the problem sheet.

After spending some time making sense of the problem and what we mean by a model, discuss ideas for making good use of a legacy.

- What things should the money be spent on? [large or small projects; long-term or short-term impacts]
- Why would the ex-pupil want the money to have a long-term impact? [so that they can see what is happening in the school over a long period; they do not want the money spent on a one-off thing …]
- What is the importance of inflation in any model we try? [money is worth less as time goes on]
- Why would you invest the money? [to make more money; to make the money last]

Main part of the unit

Note that models on the red tabs on the spreadsheet are identical to those on the corresponding green tabs but use absolute referencing to enable you to quickly change values if needed during the discussions. Alternatively, any of the sheets may be used by pupils as they investigate.

Use the sheet 'Double'.

- What do the formulae in each cell do?
- How long do you think it would take for the money to double? [18 years; extend the spreadsheet to check]

Discuss doubling for different interest rates and amend the spreadsheet to test out hypotheses.

- Would an interest rate of 8% mean the money would double in half the time? Why do you think this?

Spend plenty of time on the examples 'Model one' and 'Inflation', examining how they have been constructed. Look at:

- how to change the interest rate;
- how (on the 'Inflation' sheet) the formula can be adapted to change the annual expenditure to take account of inflation;
- why no interest has been added at the end of the first year. [Because it has been added at the start of the second year and is based on the balance assuming that the expenditure is made at the beginning of any year the interest is paid at the end – though the model could have been constructed differently.]

Look at each of the models (A to E) on the spreadsheet. Discuss what each model is aiming to do and how they differ.

- What variables can you change in each sheet?

Ask pupils to work in pairs and investigate one of the five models. As some of the models are more complex than others you may wish to allocate them to particular pairs.

Hand out the resource sheets for each model and explain that the main aim is to present a recommendation to the school on the merits, and weaknesses, of that model. As a whole class you will decide which one to recommend to the headteacher and governors. Explain that some ideas for exploration are given on each resource sheet. Pupils should prepare to include in a presentation to the class:

- assumptions they made (e.g. inflation rates and interest rates);
- what the particular strengths and weaknesses of their model are.

They are to act like consultants and make a recommendation for or against their model with a sound argument.

Towards the end of the unit pairs of pupils working on the same model combine to decide on a joint presentation of their findings.

Plenary

Each group presents their recommendations to the whole class, who then agree on a recommendation to make to the headteacher.

Solution notes

There is no right answer to this problem. A group of pupils may put a very strong case for what might appear to be a weaker model. This would be an ideal opportunity to discuss the implications this has for the way we respond to advertising and marketing in our everyday lives.

Remains of a power

Modelling and optimisation

Prerequisite knowledge
- Powers beyond squares

Why do this unit?
An initial attack on the problem with a calculator or spreadsheet fails. Eventually an indirect approach proves to be a way in. The spreadsheet offers an interactive environment in which to explore the extension ideas within the main problem.

Time
One or two lessons

Resources
CD-ROM: spreadsheet, problem sheet
NRICH website (optional):
www.nrich.maths.org, January 1998,
'Big powers'

Remains of a power

Problem sheet

What is the remainder when 2^{2002} is divided by 7?

Maths Trails: Excel at Problem Solving | Problem and resource sheets   © Cambridge University Press 2008

Introducing the unit

Is 2048 divisible by 7?

(The divisor 7 is used here but a smaller, easier number would do just as well.)

- How do you know you are right? [Division on a calculator produces a decimal.]

- How can you find the remainder if you are allowed to use a calculator? [Divide 2048 by 7 to produce a whole number followed by a decimal part. Subtract the whole number to leave just the decimal. Multiply the decimal by 7 to get the remainder, which is 4.]

Give pupils time to find remainders for other numbers.

A spreadsheet can do this very effectively using the MOD function (MOD gives the remainder when the first value is divided by the second). Demonstrate this to the group on a blank sheet

(see 'MOD help' on the spreadsheet). Then use this sheet to check remainders for 2048 and the other numbers used by pupils.

Main part of the unit

Introduce pupils to the problem from the problem sheet.

- Will a calculator help? [No, because the number is too big.]

If needed, give pupils time to try using a calculator to see why this is not helpful.

- Will a spreadsheet help? [No, for the same reason.]

Allow time for the difficulty of the task to register with pupils. Invite general thoughts about the problem and possible approaches to it. Eventually, but not too quickly, nudge pupils towards starting simply, looking systematically

40 | **Maths Trails: Excel at Problem Solving** | **Teacher's File**

at remainders for 2^1, 2^2, 2^3, 2^4, 2^5, ... Invite them to produce a table of results such as:

	2^1	2^2	2^3	2^4	2^5	2^6	...
	2	4	8	16	32	64	...
Remainder	2	4	1	2	4	1	...

- Has that helped? How? [If the powers progress systematically we might see a pattern or might see how each answer follows from the one before.]

Show the group the sheet 'Remainder – 1' on the spreadsheet and ask pupils how that helps. [There is a pattern in the remainders: 2, 4, 1 repeats forever.]

- How do we know that this pattern does continue forever? [When a value is doubled its remainder on division by 7 is also doubled. 1 becomes 2, and 2 becomes 4. 4 doubles to 8 which has a remainder of 1 when divided by 7.]

Discuss how the sheet is constructed. Notice how MOD is used and how the up arrow ($^$) in a formula produces powers.

At this point ask pupils to construct their own version of the sheet, discussing the process in whatever detail is necessary. As they complete the sheet draw their attention back to the original problem.

In pairs, pupils decide on an answer which they can justify and share with the whole group. [667 cycles of 2, 4, 1 takes us to 2^{2001} so 2^{2002}

divided by 7 has a remainder of 2, the next number in the sequence.]

If time allows ask pupils to pose problems of their own and to start looking for a solution to a more general case. They will report on their findings in the plenary in the form of posters. For example they might investigate:

- What happens for powers of 3, 4, 5, ...? Can you see and explain any generalisations?
- What happens when you divide by numbers other than 7?

'Remainder – 2' on the spreadsheet may help.

Allow plenty of time for pupils to explore and make progress with their questions. Some pupils can be invited to notice how long a cycle is and also which numbers occur as remainders and which do not.

Remember, being able to account for the pattern is the real solution.

Plenary

Invite pupils to present interesting results and ideas from their exploration using posters or an ICT-based presentation tool.

Draw attention to the way in which the spreadsheet takes the burden of calculation and leaves us to explore the mathematics.

Discuss how a single initial question led to a deeper and wider investigation. Offer the pupils useful vocabulary by referring to that bigger field as the mathematical 'structure'.

Solution notes

When 2^{2002} is divided by 7 the remainder is 2. The sheet 'Remainder – 2' on the spreadsheet may be used to verify more general results.

Power crazy

Modelling and optimisation

Prerequisite knowledge
- Powers higher than cube

Why do this unit?
There is a surprising structure and pupils can move quickly into the problem-solving process of accounting for pattern. For example, can what is true for the $3-7$ combination be explained and generalised?

Time
One lesson

Resources
Calculators
CD-ROM: spreadsheet, problem sheets 1 and 2
NRICH website (optional):
www.nrich.maths.org, June 2002, 'Power crazy'; November 2003, 'What an odd fact(or)'

Introducing the unit

Show the group the 'Power crazy' problem on problem sheet 1.

Ask the class how they would approach the first part of the problem.

- Where might you start? [Try some numbers, checking that 3 and 7 are raised to the same power.]

As pupils work individually, record their results in a table that they can all refer to. For example:

n	3^n	7^n	$3^n + 7^n$	Multiple of 10?
1	3	7	10	√
2	9	49	58	×
3	27	343	370	√
4	81	2401	2482	×
5	243	16807	17050	√
...	...	...	...	...
...	...	...	...	...

- Can we answer the question yet? [For the data available, it always appears to work for odd powers.]
- Do we know why? [The main part of the lesson explores this.]

Main part of the unit

Show the group the sheet 'Power crazy 1' on the spreadsheet. Briefly look at the contents of cells to see how the spreadsheet was created.

- What can you see? [patterns in the units digits; for example the units digit for powers of 3 follows a cycle 3, 9, 7, 1, 3, ...]
- Can you say why you know these cycles continue? [Multiplying a number with a units digit of 3 by 3 will always give you a number with a units digit of 9 and then multiplying by 3 again will give a units digit of 7. One more time brings you back to a units digit of 1. A similar argument can be used with the pattern of the units digits in powers of 7.]

Draw out the connection between the values in the two columns and how you know that the cycle of multiples of 10 will continue. That is, in both patterns the units digit has a cycle of 4 with the 3s and 7s in the units column alternating but summing to make a multiple of 10.

- What other pairs of numbers do you think this might work with? [complements of 10: 1, 9; 2, 8; 4, 6]

Explain to pupils that they are to make the spreadsheet, first with 3 and 7 and then with other combinations. They may wish to copy tables so they have a record to refer to. Divide the class into three groups, each focusing on and justifying their results for one of the other three combinations [1, 9; 2, 8 and 4, 6]. Each group should create a poster for display and prepare to present their explanation to the rest of the class in the plenary.

Extension

You may wish to leave the group with the challenge of what other pairs of numbers generate which multiples – for example which, if any, powers of 3 and 2 will give multiples of 5.

Plenary

Have pupils present and discuss their justifications. This is an ideal opportunity for peer evaluation – which explanation did the group like the best and why?

If time allows, the group can explore the problem 'What an odd fact(or)' on problem sheet 2 to reinforce this style of reasoning.

Solution notes

Power crazy

The justification for multiples of 10 using the properties of cycles is more than adequate.

What an odd fact(or)

The sum can be rewritten as $(1^{99} + 9^{99}) + (2^{99} + 8^{99}) + (3^{99} + 7^{99}) + (4^{99} + 6^{99}) + 5^{99}$. Each bracket contains a multiple of 10 – from the arguments in the main part of the lesson – and you are adding a multiple of 5 so the total must be a multiple of 5.

Further ideas

Expand $x^n + (10 - x)^n$ to see why odd values of n will produce a result that has 10 as a factor. Allow the '10' to become a variable to generalise for multiples other than 10.

Left overs

Modelling and optimisation

Prerequisite knowledge
- Common factors and common multiples

Why do this unit?
The spreadsheet prompts the solver to see there is an underpinning structure to this problem context. It is up to the pupils to explain the structure and make use of it. For example, can the interval of 60 between solutions be explained and generalised?

Time
Two lessons

Resources
CD-ROM: spreadsheet, problem sheets 1 and 2

NRICH website (optional): www.nrich.maths.org, November 1996, 'Remainders'; March 2007, 'The Chinese remainder theorem'

Left overs

Problem sheet 1

Sweets

When the contents of a jar of sweets are divided into two equal piles, one sweet is left over. If that same jar is divided into three, four, five or six equal piles, the remainder would still be one in every case. How many sweets are there?
- Is a solution possible?
- Is there more than one solution?
- Was the result predictable?

Introducing the unit

Show pupils 'Sweets' on problem sheet 1.

- Where would you start? What should we try? [Try some numbers.]

- Is a solution possible? Can you explain why this is so?

Have pupils work on their own for a few minutes, trying some numbers and recording any results and insights. After a short time stop the group. Share and draw out pointers to the structure of the problem. For example, the number of sweets must be odd (this leaves one when divided by 2) and must be one more than a multiple of 3, so already the possibilities are constrained (7, 13, 19, ...).

- Can we use this idea about multiples? [We can be more particular in the numbers we try. We also need the number of sweets to be one more than a multiple of 4, of 5 and of 6.]

Allow a short period in which pupils, working in pairs, continue to calculate and think. End the introduction ready to move into finding a solution or, if one has been found, pose the question:

- Could there be more than one solution?

Main part of the unit

Show pupils the sheet 'Plain sweets' on the spreadsheet.

Invite pupils to say what calculation is being done from looking at the numbers, and then click each cell to see the formula used and discuss the MOD function. [MOD gives the remainder when the first value is divided by the second. MOD(17, 3) would give 2 because when 17 is divided by 3 there is a remainder of 2.]

Take time throughout the following stages of the unit for mental arithmetic or calculator use if that is helpful.

- How would you recognise a solution in the spreadsheet? [a row of ones]

Scan down and ask pupils to look for a solution. Finding the row of ones is easy but we can make this even easier by using **conditional formatting**. Show the group the sheet 'Sweets' on the spreadsheet and briefly discuss what the conditional formatting is doing. [highlighting a cell which contains the value 1]

- The sheet starts at 80. Is 80 a good start value? [No, because there may be solutions less than 80.]

Discuss what would be better. Change the 80 to 1, drawing attention to the formula, for example =B3+1 in cell B4, which causes automatic recalculation. Scan down and record solutions as they occur.

- What do you notice? [Rows of ones appear at intervals of 60.]
- Was that interval predictable? [Solutions in intervals must be a multiple of 2, and a multiple of 3 and 4 and 5 and 6 – that is, the common multiple of 2, 3, 4, 5, and 6.]
- What is the first solution? [1] Why is that a solution? [Each pile receives no sweets with one left over.]

Encourage discussion, relating ways of expressing a general solution [any multiple of 60, plus 1] to the original problem.

Show the group the problem 'Remainders' on problem sheet 2.

Explain to pupils that they will be expected to produce their own spreadsheets and to justify their solutions to the rest of the group at the end of the session. Ask pupils to plan on paper before they move to the computer to use Excel.

The following prompts may be useful while the pupils are working:

- What formula did you need in each cell? [use MOD for remainders, a formula to create the first column values]
- What will you be looking for in the rows? [1, 2, ...]
- Can you convince me that you have found the smallest number that works?

Plenary

Use examples from the pupil-produced spreadsheets to discuss results and insights including the value of using a spreadsheet and the efficiency of different layouts. The sheets 'Plain remainders' and 'Remainders' may be useful.

- Can you explain why the solutions appear at intervals of 60? [LCM]
- Can you explain why the smallest solution is 59? [60 would have a remainder of zero for all divisors. 59 is one less than a multiple of each of the divisors, so it will leave a remainder of 5 when divided by 6, a remainder of 4 when divided by 5, and so on.]
- If the remainder had to be two less than the number you divided by what would be the smallest solution? [58]

Solution notes

For 'Sweets', the first solution is 1 and then all the other solutions follow at intervals of 60 (there is an infinite number of solutions). For 'Remainders', the first positive solution is 59 with solutions continuing in steps of 60 (again, there is an infinite set of solutions).

The article 'The Chinese remainder theorem' on the NRICH website explores the mathematics of these problems in greater depth.

Make 100

Modelling and optimisation

Prerequisite knowledge
- Formulae in a spreadsheet

Why do this unit?
The design and creation of the spreadsheet involves pupils in having a sound understanding of the mathematical context. Pupils will need to problem solve in order to produce a spreadsheet which will support them in their search for a solution.

Time
Two lessons

Resources
CD-ROM: spreadsheet, problem sheets 1 and 2

NRICH website (optional): www.nrich.maths.org, October 2005, 'Data chunks'; September 1999, 'Euclid's algorithm I'

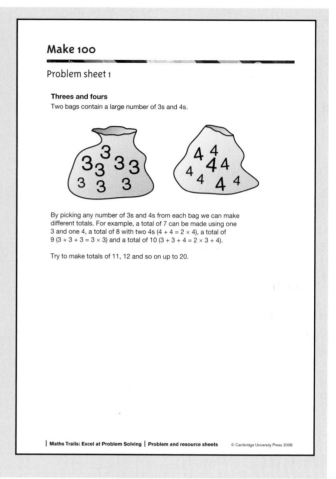

Make 100

Problem sheet 1

Threes and fours
Two bags contain a large number of 3s and 4s.

By picking any number of 3s and 4s from each bag we can make different totals. For example, a total of 7 can be made using one 3 and one 4, a total of 8 with two 4s (4 + 4 = 2 × 4), a total of 9 (3 + 3 + 3 = 3 × 3) and a total of 10 (3 + 3 + 4 = 2 × 3 + 4).

Try to make totals of 11, 12 and so on up to 20.

| Maths Trails: Excel at Problem Solving | Problem and resource sheets   © Cambridge University Press 2008

Introducing the unit

Introduce the problem 'Threes and fours' on problem sheet 1.

Collect and display successful combinations of 3s and 4s.

- What can you say about the totals? [We can make them all, and some can be made in more than one way.]
- Which ones can you do in more than one way? [12, 15, 16, 18, 19, 20]
- How do you know you have all the possible ways of making them? [We need to be systematic and try all the arrangements or find a rule.]

The next stage is to work together to develop a systematic approach, sharing findings. You will need to discuss with the group their ideas, giving them time to talk in pairs before bringing ideas together. Your aim could be to end up with a table showing all possible combinations.

This could look like:

	3	6	9	12	15	18
4	7	10	13	16	19	22
8	11	14	17	20	23	26
12	15	18	21	24	27	30
16	19	22	25	28	31	34
20	23	26	29	32	35	38

Working with tables on paper will make the structuring of the spreadsheet easier to grasp later in the activity. Note that the table above has the multiples of 4s and 3s as row and column headers so that the principal operation within the cells of the table is addition. Check that pupils understand that the table will contain every possible successful combination.

Main part of the unit

Introduce the problem 'Make 100' on problem sheet 2.

How is this problem the same as and different from the 'Threes and fours' problem? [The total is still made from threes and fours but one specific result is required, 100, and we want to know exactly how many combinations will produce that result.]

Ask the group to spend a few minutes thinking on their own about the problem and how they might solve it, before moving them into pairs to compare ideas. When ready ask the whole group to share their approaches.

Draw pupils' attention to the use of a table in the 'Threes and fours' problem and discuss how a spreadsheet might be able to help, by systematically producing all possible combinations in a two-way table.

Open the sheet '3 & 4'
- What formula would you expect to be in cell C4? [Pupils may say =C3+B4.]

Show the formula in C4. It is formed from C3 and B4 but has $ signs in front of the 3 and the B. Look at some other cells to confirm similar use of the $ sign. Explain the purpose of the dollar sign (see the sheet 'Help - Table of 2 variables'). Use sheet '3 & 4 blank' to reinforce pupils' understanding of absolute references:
- Create the formula =C$3+$B4 in cell C4.
- Select C4 and copy.
- Select the range C4:I9 and paste.

Start the pupils working on the problem and constructing their own spreadsheets. They will need to:

- plan on paper;
- implement and test their spreadsheet;
- identify solutions and notice any patterns [solutions lie along a diagonal line].

As a whole group, discuss key points including a comparison of efficiency between different designs. The sheet '3 & 4' on the spreadsheet may be helpful.

Plenary

The plenary can focus on explaining why the solutions lie on a line and how this can be used to generate all solutions.

- How are the solutions related? [Adjacent solutions are always four along and three up.]
- What does that really mean? [Moving four along is a change of four 3s (12) and moving three up is a change of three 4s (12). Replacing four 3s by three 4s, or vice versa, produces the next solution along the line.]
- Can we now use this idea to generate all the solutions without a spreadsheet? [Yes, find one solution and from that replace groups of three 4s with four 3s, and then, starting again from the original solution, replace groups of four 3s with three 4s. This is the same as moving up and down the line of solutions in the table.]

Solution notes

Make 100
There are nine combinations which make 100.

$$25 \times 4 + 0 \times 3$$
$$22 \times 4 + 4 \times 3$$
$$19 \times 4 + 8 \times 3$$
$$16 \times 4 + 12 \times 3$$
$$13 \times 4 + 16 \times 3$$
$$10 \times 4 + 20 \times 3$$
$$7 \times 4 + 24 \times 3$$
$$4 \times 4 + 28 \times 3$$
$$1 \times 4 + 32 \times 3$$

Different but same

Modelling and optimisation

Prerequisite knowledge

- Square of a number
- Expansion of brackets

Why do this unit?

Pupils will learn the general skill of producing a table of results from two variables, applying it here to explore algebraic equivalence. The algebraic identity used here is the difference of two squares.

Time

One lesson

Resources

CD-ROM: spreadsheet, resource sheet

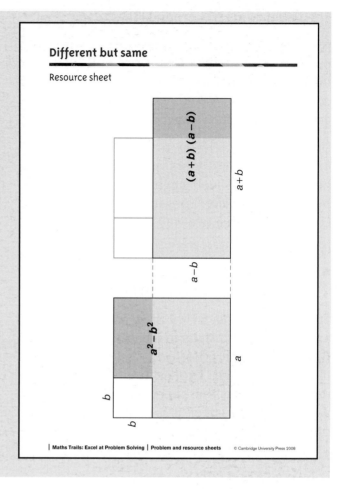

Different but same

Resource sheet

| Maths Trails: Excel at Problem Solving | Problem and resource sheets | © Cambridge University Press 2008

Introducing the unit

Show the group the sheet 'Grid 1' on the spreadsheet.

- What can you say about the red numbers? [square numbers]
- Can you see a connection between the blue numbers in the grid and the red numbers at the top and side? [sum of squares]
- Do you notice anything else, and can you account for it? [For example, the main diagonal top-left to bottom-right contains only even numbers, and parallel diagonals alternate all odd, all even. This is because two odd or two even squares produce an even sum, and an odd and an even square produce an odd sum.]

Main part of the unit

Show the group the sheet 'Grid 2' on the spreadsheet. Ask pupils to spend one minute on their own making a quick record of anything they notice. Pupils can then share in pairs, leading into a whole-group discussion which explores the patterns in diagonals or in rows and columns, as with 'Grid 1'. [For example, rows and columns show the same pattern of increase – going up in odd number steps. As well, diagonals consist of either all odd or all even numbers.]

- Do you see more than one connection between the blue numbers within the grid and the black numbers at the top and side of the grid? [a difference of squares, and a product of a sum with a difference, for example in cell K6: $8^2 - 3^2 = 55$ and also $(8+3)(8-3) = 55$]

The activity from this point forwards helps pupils to consolidate their understanding of this equivalence (that a difference of two squares is identical to the product of a sum and a difference, or in algebra:
$$a^2 - b^2 = (a + b)(a - b)).$$

This equivalence will be reinforced through:

- constructing two versions of the table, one using the differences of two squares and the other using the product of a sum and a difference;
- looking at the algebraic equivalence of the two expressions (expanding brackets);
- considering diagrammatic representations (in the plenary).

Show pupils 'Blank grid 1' on the spreadsheet. The aim is to create a table for each of the two expressions, and check that they give the same result. First create the table for the difference of two squares.

- What formula should we type for cell D4 in the first grid? [pupils may say =D3–C4]

Type this formula into D4 and press **Enter** so that pupils can see the result. So far this looks good.

Copy the formula across the whole grid.

- This does not work – why? [Look at the values in the first row: for example the 11 in G4 should have been the difference between 16 and 1 but the actual calculation was the difference between 16 and 5.]

Explain that to overcome this problem we will use **absolute references** (see the sheet 'Help - Table of 2 variables'). Demonstrate the correct formula, =D$3–$C4. Discuss the negative values that appear in the grid (use the **ABS** command if you wish to make all results positive).

We have done this calculation using square (red) numbers. But here we need to work directly with the black numbers, so display sheet 'Blank grid 2'.

Discuss and derive the formula needed in the first table (difference of two squares). [=C$2^2–$B3^2]. Explain to the group that they need to produce both tables (difference of the two squares and product of a sum and a difference) in 'Blank grid 2'. [For the product table the formula is =(O$2+$N3)*(O$2–$N3).]

Producing grids with absolute references can be a demanding task. Judge when to draw pupils into discussion on issues relating to the process or understanding as they arise. When pupils have completed both grids move into the plenary, where a connection can be made with algebraic and/or diagrammatic representations of the relationship.

Plenary

- Why do you think the two grids contain the same numbers? [The formulae are equivalent – pupils might say 'We are doing the same thing in a different way'.]

Show and discuss the diagrammatic presentation of equivalence offered on the resource sheet and connect that with the 'traditional' algebraic approach involving the expansion of brackets.

Solution notes

$a^2 – b^2 = (a+b)(a-b)$

Tree tops

Modelling and optimisation

Prerequisite knowledge
- Experience of producing a model using a spreadsheet
- Formulae in a spreadsheet

Why do this unit?
Interpreting the information given on the problem sheet is a significant part of this activity. The problem encourages pupils to experiment with different models. Very basic ideas can lead quickly to useful outcomes and encourage pupils to extend their models. The use of the spreadsheet can encourage a systematic approach to variation and reduce calculations.

Time
Two lessons

Resources
CD-ROM: spreadsheet, problem sheet
NRICH website (optional):
www.nrich.maths.org, June 2003, 'Tree tops'

Tree tops

Problem sheet

A manager of a forestry company in Scotland has to decide which trees to plant. There are three main species to choose from: Sitka Spruce, European Larch or Lodgepole Pine.

Whatever trees are planted they have to be thinned after 10 and 20 years, and the wood from the thinning is sold for a profit.

Sitha spruce   European larch   Lodgepole pine

Each kind of tree has a different planting cost per hectare, a different growth rate and a different value per hectare depending on the age the tree is felled. All this information is given in the table below.

	Sitka Spruce	European Larch	Lodgepole Pine
Planting cost per hectare (£)	120 000	115 000	130 000
Profit per hectare from 10 years thin (£)	10 000	15 000	20 000
Profit per hectare from 20 years thin (£)	40 000	40 000	30 000

	Possible income per hectare		
Growing period (years)	(£)	(£)	(£)
30	358 000	192 000	122 500
40	513 000	469 200	366 400
50	693 000	858 000	646 000
60	834 000	1 184 000	950 200
70	1 126 800	1 158 000	1 144 000
80	904 000	1 059 000	1 310 800
90	805 000	837 000	1 476 000

What strategy for planting and felling would you recommend to the manager in order to maximise the profit:
- after 70 years?
- after 90 years?
- more generally?

Introducing the unit

Present the problem given on the problem sheet.

Ask the pupils to spend a few minutes on their own making sense of the problem, writing notes if it helps them clarify their ideas. After two or three minutes, ask pupils to talk in pairs about what they have noticed and what they might try first, telling them that you will want to share their ideas in five minutes…
Think – Pair – Share

The aim is for pupils to notice issues such as a planting of 20 years or less is not profitable and the minimum time for trees to grow and make a profit needs to be 30 years.

Gather ideas and make a list (including the 30-year minimum time for a profit) of possible ways forward on the board. For example:

- Find the profits for each type of tree after 30, 40, 50 years.

- Find the profits for two plantings of a given species over 70, 80, 90, 100 years. (Note that there are only a limited number of possibilities here: 70 = 30 + 40; 80 = 30 + 50 or 40 + 40; 90 = 30 + 60 or 40 + 50; 100 = 30 + 70 or 40 + 60 or 50 + 50 – see 'One species, two plantings' on the spreadsheet).

- Find the profits for two plantings of two different species.

Main part of the unit

Introduce the sheet 'Data' on the spreadsheet. Using the idea of the potential profits from single plantings, invite pupils, in pairs, to discuss, plan and implement a spreadsheet to calculate profits for different time spans. Remind them that they need to produce evidence to support the advice they would give to the manager.

- What will you need to include on your spreadsheet? [how much it costs to plant, the profits from each thinning and the felling, totals for each of the trees for 30, 40, …, 90 years]

Remind pupils that their aim is to present a spreadsheet clearly so that it explains why they are making their recommendation to the manager. As they finish each model they should write their recommendation at the bottom of the sheet, add their names and print it for discussion at the end of the lesson.

As pairs finish the single planting model and are able to make a recommendation, ask them to consider a more complex model of mixed planting over different periods. Again have pupils print their recommendations for discussion later.

During this part of the activity identify models that can inform the discussion in the plenary. For example, models that:

- are elegantly represented using a spreadsheet;
- show a systematic approach;
- are giving high profits based on multiple plantings of one tree species or mixed planting for discussion in the plenary.

Pupils who are struggling with producing models of their own may find it helpful to use the models started in the sheets 'One species, one planting' and 'One species, two plantings' on the spreadsheet (green tabs). If using the prepared spreadsheets, pupils will need to spend time making sense of the model.

Prior to the plenary ask pairs to choose one of their models to share.

Plenary

Have pairs of pupils swap models and talk about their findings. Ask pairs if they were given models and recommendations they were particularly impressed with (or use one or two models you have identified). Discuss what makes these good examples and how they might be improved further, for example by planting more species. Other ideas might include considering mixed plantings so that you could get profits in the shorter and longer term and reduce risk of problems (e.g. disease) that might arise from planting just one species.

Solution notes

It you were to plant a single species, the most profitable tree after 50 years is the Sitka Spruce, but after 70 years it is the European Larch and, for 80 years or more, the Lodgepole Pine.

After 70 years some trees are losing value and after 90 years all trees are losing value.

A better strategy might be to plant the same species successively for less time. For example, two 50-year plantings of Sitka Spruce gives a higher return than any single planting over 100 years. Alternatively, mixing the species and planting for different periods may be more profitable – for example, over 90 years, 30 years of Sitka Spruce and 60 years of European Larch (see 'One species models' on the spreadsheet).

The parcel

Modelling and optimisation

Prerequisite knowledge
- Nets and volumes of cuboids
- Formulae in a spreadsheet
- Construction of two-way tables
- Absolute referencing (optional)

Why do this unit?
The aim is to model a situation to obtain a solution using trial and improvement. An initial task gives pupils time to become familiar with the setting for the second task by deconstructing a ready-made spreadsheet.

Time
One or two lessons

Resources
Individual whiteboards, a cuboid
CD-ROM: spreadsheet, problem sheets 1 and 2, resource sheets 1–3
NRICH website (optional):
www.nrich.maths.org, January 2005, 'Sending a parcel'; July 2006, 'All wrapped up';
a number of optimisation problems were published in January 2005 including 'Fence it' (knowledge of area and perimeter of rectangles), 'Where to land' (requires Pythagoras' theorem) and 'Slippage' (requires some knowledge of trigonometry)

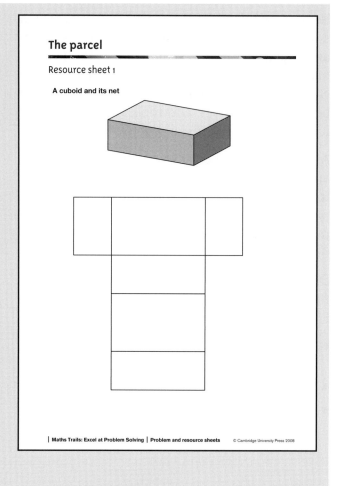

The parcel

Resource sheet 1

A cuboid and its net

| Maths Trails: Excel at Problem Solving | Problem and resource sheets   © Cambridge University Press 2008

Introducing the unit

The main objective of the introduction is to ensure pupils' confidence with the net(s) of a cuboid and the relationship between the dimensions of a cube and the measurements on a net – see resource sheet 1.

Show the class a cuboid.

- How many faces, edges and vertices does it have? [6, 12, 8]

Ask pupils to draw a net on their whiteboards or on paper. Discuss the equivalence of the different nets pupils have drawn. Ask pupils to select one edge and mark all the edges on their net that are the same length.

- How many different edge lengths are there? [3 – height, length and width]

Use the image on resource sheet 1 to establish how the width and the length of the net are made of three and four edge lengths respectively (see resource sheets 2 and 3 for examples).

Ensure pupils are comfortable with the relationship between the dimensions of a cuboid and the net before moving on to the main part of the unit.

Main part of the unit

This is in two parts. The first involves deconstructing the sheet 'Wrapping presents' and the second part involves getting pupils to construct their own spreadsheet.

Show pupils the problem 'Wrapping presents' (problem sheet 1), which involves finding the largest cuboid that can be covered completely with a sheet of A3 paper. Ask them to spend a few minutes on their own trying to make sense of the problem, perhaps by drawing a diagram, and thinking about how they might go about finding a solution if they had a spreadsheet.

After a short time ask pupils to talk to a partner about their ideas and get ready to share thoughts with the rest of the class. It is worth spending some time while the pairs are working 'harvesting' some ideas to use in the next part of the lesson if suggestions are not forthcoming.

Share ideas with the whole class before looking at the spreadsheet 'Wrapping presents'. You might, however, prefer to construct the spreadsheet from scratch by talking through some of the ideas with the class, especially if pupils have come up with equally valid but quite different approaches. Examples of different approaches (including using spinners and two-way tables) can be found in the spreadsheets 'Parcel basic', 'Parcel with control for height', 'Parcel with spinner for height' and 'Parcel two-way table'.

- How was this sheet constructed? [Height is increasing by 1 unit, width and length are determined by the dimensions of the paper – see the diagrams on the spreadsheet.]
- What is the purpose of the spreadsheet? [It calculates lengths and widths from given heights and then calculates the volume.]
- Why are there two tables? [two orientations of the A3 sheet – see resource sheets 2 and 3]

- How does it help with finding a solution? [By scanning the Volume column it is easy to identify the maximum, 1512 cm^3, for both orientations (is that surprising?).]

Having spent time deconstructing the spreadsheet – building confidence both in its construction and how it relates to the original task and the net – pupils should be ready to tackle the task 'Sending a parcel' (problem sheet 2) in pairs. This problem also requires pupils to find a maximum volume but with different constraints. Remind pupils to plan what they will do with the spreadsheet before they start, checking their understanding of the problem after a few minutes.

Pupils who are finding the ideas difficult may wish to use the spreadsheet 'Parcel' to get started. Their aim will be to extend the table and create new tables with different heights, homing in on a solution.

Things to look out for:

- Some pupils may struggle with the need to deal with two variables – how could they do this systematically? [Keep one variable constant to start with and vary the other.]
- Some pupils may wish to use the idea of two-way tables and may need support with absolute referencing to do this.

Plenary

Discuss the different methods adopted by the group and their solutions. Key points to draw out include how their models enabled the groups to home in on solutions and why the use of a spreadsheet aided efficiency.

Solution notes

The maximum volume for part 2 of the problem is 74 052 cm^3 if the dimensions of the parcel are in cm (see the spreadsheet).

Under the ribbon

Modelling and optimisation

Prerequisite knowledge
- Pythagoras' theorem

Why do this unit?
Here the spreadsheet gives access to a problem where the algebraic approach could prove difficult. The answer to the problem is surprising.

Time
One lesson

Resources
Ribbon, metre rulers, drawing pins and plastic construction cubes
CD-ROM: spreadsheet, resource sheet, problem sheet
NRICH website (optional): www.nrich.maths.org, January 2005, 'Slippage'; November 2007, 'Under the ribbon'

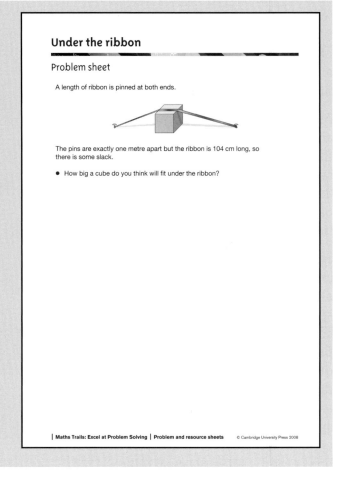

Under the ribbon

Problem sheet

A length of ribbon is pinned at both ends.

The pins are exactly one metre apart but the ribbon is 104 cm long, so there is some slack.

- How big a cube do you think will fit under the ribbon?

| Maths Trails: Excel at Problem Solving | Problem and resource sheets   © Cambridge University Press 2008

Introducing the unit

Introduce the group to the problem 'Under the ribbon' on the problem sheet.

- How big a cube do you think will fit under the ribbon?

Record pupils' estimations for later.

Direct the group to experiment with real ribbon and cubes of different sizes to arrive at a confirmation of their estimate or to settle on a revised value.

- Where is it best to place the cube? [centre]
- What is your estimate now? [record new estimates]
- What could we change about the experiment to get a more accurate answer to the main question? [Use smaller cubes, use more accurate measuring equipment.]

This last question leads towards finding an answer by calculation.

Main part of the unit

Explain to pupils that to clarify their thinking they will use their calculators to work through a single calculation based on their estimates.

Show diagram A from the resource sheet to help pupils visualise the situation.

- What do we know? [100 cm between the pins and ribbon length of 104 cm]
- What do we want to find? [the cube size that fits under a ribbon length of 104 cm]

Discuss what is known in relation to what is wanted and draw pupils towards seeing the possible value of using Pythagoras' theorem.

However, we do not appear to have sufficient information as the 'sloping length' of the ribbon depends on the height of the cube. So we need to estimate a height for the cube and use that to work out a length for the ribbon.

Discuss the merits of a spreadsheet when

approaching a problem which requires trial and improvement in the search for a solution.

In diagrams B and C on the resource sheet the estimate for the sake of discussion has been taken as 6 cm.

Starting with our estimate for the length of the side of the cube we can find the shortest length of ribbon that this cube could fit under.

- If we calculate the ribbon length with our estimate for the cube size, would it be 104 cm? [Probably not. If an estimate is too low the calculated length of the ribbon will be less than 104 cm and this tells us we need to try a larger cube. If our calculation gives a ribbon length greater than 104 cm we know our estimate for the cube is too high.]
- What is the calculation we need to do? [Using diagram C and working with a cube side of 6 cm we can calculate the hypotenuse and use this to find the length of the ribbon.]

Ask pupils to make the calculation using their own estimate. Ask them to suggest an improved second value for the cube side.

Explain that a row in a spreadsheet can work like the calculation they have just done.

Pupils need to discuss and plan their own spreadsheet. There may come a point in this process where you may find it helpful to show pupils the sheet 'Finding the cube side' on the spreadsheet. This can be deconstructed and an explanation given of each formula that has been used.

In this sheet the first column shows cube sides being tested. These advance in equal steps. The final column shows the full ribbon length passing over that cube. This needs to be 104 cm. Cell B5 can be changed to give an improved starting value, and the formula in cell B6 can be adjusted to give a small step size, finer increments giving an increasingly more accurate value for the length of the side of the cube.

Pupils need to implement their own designs, or replicate, or use the sheet 'Finding the cube side'.

When the groups have made progress, return to whole-group discussion. Compare solutions and the effectiveness of different methods.

Plenary

The calculation so far has been based on a cube placed at the centre but this is an assumption that it might be useful to revisit.

- For a specific cube size is the length of ribbon shortest when the cube is centred on 50 cm? [Yes. See the sheet 'Testing the centre position'.]

In 'Testing the centre position' on the spreadsheet you can change the cube side length in cell B4. The left section length increases from 0 to 100 in steps of 1 cm. We need to scan down column I to see where the shortest length of ribbon appears [when the cube is centred at 50 cm, that is, 47 cm from one end for a 6 cm cube].

Solution notes

The side of the cube is 13.3 cm (to 3 s.f.). Surprised?

The fire-fighter

Modelling and optimisation

Prerequisite knowledge
● Pythagoras' theorem

Why do this unit?
This activity will reinforce the use of a spreadsheet for optimisation problems. Pupils are required to use what they have learned in the first part of the problem to help them solve the second part.

Time
Two lessons

Resources
A length of string, a couple of drawing pins and some keys on a key ring
CD-ROM: spreadsheet, problem sheet, resource sheets 1 and 2
NRICH website (optional): www.nrich.maths.org, January 2005, 'Where to land'; November 2007, 'The fire-fighter's car keys'

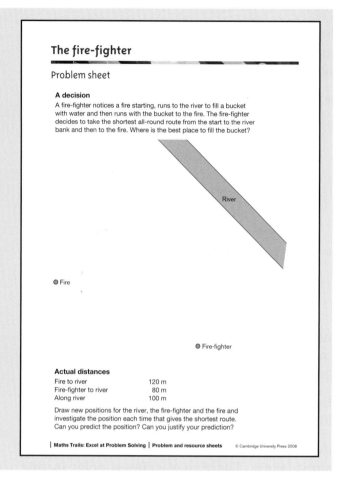

The fire-fighter

Problem sheet

A decision
A fire-fighter notices a fire starting, runs to the river to fill a bucket with water and then runs with the bucket to the fire. The fire-fighter decides to take the shortest all-round route from the start to the river bank and then to the fire. Where is the best place to fill the bucket?

River

Fire

Fire-fighter

Actual distances

Fire to river	120 m
Fire-fighter to river	80 m
Along river	100 m

Draw new positions for the river, the fire-fighter and the fire and investigate the position each time that gives the shortest route. Can you predict the position? Can you justify your prediction?

| Maths Trails: Excel at Problem Solving | Problem and resource sheets   © Cambridge University Press 2008

Introducing the unit

Show the group the problem on the problem sheet. This requires pupils to find the shortest distance to a fire via a river, to collect water. Pupils will need their own copy of the problem sheet for individual work.

● What does 'shortest all-round route' mean? [There are two parts to the route: towards the river, then away from the river to the fire. The combined distance needs to be a minimum.]

Discuss with pupils how they might find the position along the river bank which will give the minimum distance by using a ruler and trial and improvement.

● How can we define this point? [Suggest that the distance can be measured from the nearest point on the river to the fire-fighter – point A on resource sheet 1.]

The diagram may distort slightly in the process of printing or photocopying but for the first part of the activity this is not a problem.

Give pupils a few minutes to find the 'optimal' position through measurement and trial and improvement, and share findings.

● How could we improve accuracy? [use Pythagoras' theorem]

Main part of the unit

Show the group the sheet 'River start' on the spreadsheet and spend some time making sense of the way the sheet is constructed. [The sheet calculates the total distance from the fire-fighter to the fire via the river based on the diagrams on the problem and resource sheets with $d = 100$ mm, $a = 80$ mm and $b = 120$ mm (a nominal scale of 1 mm to 1 m).]

Check that the use of Pythagoras' theorem and the **SQRT** function in Excel is clear. For example, the Excel formula =SQRT(49) would return the value 7.

Take pupils through the process of scanning down the 'Combined distance' column to locate the minimum value and the position between A and B where this occurs. If some pupils suggest that the ratio split of AB matches the ratio of $a:b$ ask the group if that can be justified as a general result. If not, suggest that more examples could be useful and move to the second activity where pupils create, measure and record their own results.

Encourage pupils to try different positions for the river, the fire and the fire-fighter, keeping the distance along the river a constant (100 mm in their scale say, as this will make comparisons of results easier).

- What might you record? [The distance of the best position along the bank from a fixed point (for example the nearest point on the river to the fire-fighter), and distances from the fire and from the fire-fighter directly to the river – see lengths a and b on resource sheet 1.]

Record the findings for different lengths and distances and discuss any conjectures pupils might have about the best place on the river to run to. [For example, the further the fire-fighter is from the river, the further up the river towards the fire he will need to aim for. The distance along the river seems to be linked closely to the distances the fire-fighter and fire are from the river.]

By changing the values for the distances a and b in cells A2 and A3 in 'River' on the spreadsheet, results can be checked. The minimum is automatically picked out. Note in particular the use of absolute references (e.g. A1) in this sheet.

If time allows, pupils can make their own versions of the sheets 'River start' and 'River', but if the sheets are used as ready-made utilities pupils still need to visualise the route. Return to the diagram to confirm results as necessary.

Pupils may begin to see possible relationships and start to justify what they see without too much prompting but there is likely to be a need

to focus discussion.

- Is there any connection between the a and b values and the position on AB which produces the shortest route?
- What might be useful a, b values to try? [For example one approach could be to explore $a = 2b$ for different values of a, then restart using other multiples of b.]
- Can you justify any of your conjectures? [The diagram in resource sheet 2 shows an equivalent problem with a much simpler solution – if the fire-fighter ran the same distance to the river edge but from the other side of the river (assuming the river has no width), the best position to fill the bucket would be on that line so that the overall route was a straight line. This means that the two triangles are similar and so the ratio of corresponding sides confirms the fact that the best point along the river divides d in the ratio $a:b$.]

Plenary

On a pin board mark a horizontal line and then, some way above the left-hand side of the line, push in one pin. Push in the other pin at a different height above the line towards the right-hand side. Put a length of string through a key ring. Place the ends of the string one over each pin so that the keys hang above the line. Explain that you will slowly release the string so that the keys cross the line.

- Can you predict the position where the keys will cross the line?

Invite pupils to put a pin at the predicted point. Discuss the general relationship between the position of the pins and the point where the keys cross.

- How is this problem related to the fire-fighter activity? [It reduces to a shortest route problem.]

Use the sheet 'Car keys' on the spreadsheet to confirm hypotheses.

Solution notes

The required position is located as follows: if the point on the river's edge nearest the fire-fighter (A) is a distance a from the fire-fighter, and the point on the river's edge nearest the fire (B) is a distance b from the fire, then the shortest route uses a point that splits AB in the proportion $a:b$.

The keys will slip to hang as low as possible for any given length of string. They will touch the line where the route from pin to line to other pin is a minimum. They touch the line at this point rather than any other point because the increased string length available for any other position would have allowed the keys to hang somewhere lower than the line and they would slip to do so.

Cola can

Modelling and optimisation

Prerequisite knowledge
- Area of a rectangle and of a circle
- Volume of a cylinder

Why do this unit?
This problem utilises a spreadsheet to aid optimisation and demonstrates the value of a graph to support analysis.

Time
Two lessons

Resources
A sample of tins or cans of different sizes and proportions
CD-ROM: spreadsheet, resource sheets 1–8 (six rectangles can be made into cylinders using paper clips; solution cylinder)
NRICH website (optional):
www.nrich.maths.org, July 2007, 'Gutter'; November 2007, 'Cola can'

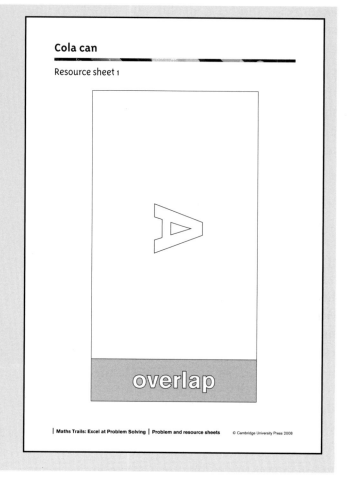

Cola can

Resource sheet 1

A

overlap

| Maths Trails: Excel at Problem Solving | Problem and resource sheets   © Cambridge University Press 2008

Introducing the unit

This unit is about creating a cylinder with a given volume that has the smallest possible surface area.

Show pupils the six cylinders made from the resource sheets.

- Which is the smallest? Which is the largest?

Include orderings based on the impression of volume and of surface area. First, working with surface area:

- How can we calculate the surface areas? [Find the area of the rectangle each cylinder was created from.]

Unwrap each cylinder to help illustrate the calculation and make measurements, or use the heights and widths given on the 'Dimension sheet' on resource sheet 7.

Compare the order based on calculations with the order based on impressions and discuss.

Now ask pupils to estimate the volumes of the cylinders A through to F from the resource sheets.

- How can we calculate those volumes? [Discussion might include recalling the volume formula, or deriving the formula by visualising a base area multiplied by height, as for a general prism.]
- What do we need to know? [radius]
- How can we find that? [Draw out the relationship between the width of the rectangle, the circumference and the radius of the cylinder.]

Calculate the radii and then the volumes of the cylinders.

Compare the new ordering based on calculation with the initial ordering made by impression.

Draw particular attention to the three cylinders that have similar volume but which were made from rectangles with different areas.

Main part of the unit

Show pupils a sample of commercially produced tins and cans. Discuss the value of minimising packaging materials.

A cola drink manufacturer has to keep costs low and might try to use as little aluminium as possible for the can.

- Can this be worked out? [If the volume is known (a cola can has a volume of 330 ml or 330 cm^3) a range of cylinders with different radii and heights can be made with that volume and it is then possible to calculate their surface areas.]

Ask pupils for a radius–height combination that they think might work for a volume 330 cm^3, or come close. Calculate the volume with the whole group. Invite suggestions for improved radius or height values. Ask pupils to make further calculations to improve their results. Draw out the advantages of increasing or decreasing just one of the variables and keeping the other fixed.

Take radius–height values from pupils which gave volume results close to 330 cm^3 and use these to calculate surface areas (including the bases and tops of the cans).

- Why is this approach to finding a minimum surface area inefficient? [Because even if the volume is close to 330 m^3, we have made many calculations without knowing if we have found the best (minimum) result for the surface area.]

If it does not arise naturally out of discussion, explain that it isn't necessary to guess both the radius and the height. If we know one of these we can work out the other using the volume of 330 cm^3.

- If we take a radius value of 10 cm, what will be the height? What is the complete surface area for this can? [0.525 cm, 661 cm^2 (both 3 s.f.)]

- If we take a height value of 10 cm, what will be the radius? What is the complete surface area? [3.24 cm, 270 cm^2 (both to 3 s.f.)]

Remind the group that the aim is to make the surface area as small as possible.

We could adjust the radius of 10 cm to get closer to the minimum surface area and continue until we are satisfied that we are close enough. However, these calculations can be done very efficiently on a spreadsheet.

Discuss with the group the possible structure of a suitable spreadsheet to do this before they attempt their own constructions, or use 'Changing the radius' on the spreadsheet as a prompt. Pupils will need to satisfy themselves that the formula in each cell performs the required calculation. In particular, look in column F (total surface area): the values in cells F6 to F8 suggest a revised start value of 3 and an increment of 0.1 (say). Further iterations of this process will continue to improve the accuracy of the result.

Instead of adjusting the radius it is possible to adjust the height – see the sheet 'Changing the height' on the spreadsheet.

Plenary

Graphs offer a valuable aid to visualisation. The sheet 'Changing the radius (graph)' on the spreadsheet contains a graph which shows the relationship between choice of radius and the resulting surface area. See also 'Changing the height (graph)'.

The sheet 'Graph help' explains how a graph can be created in Excel. Demonstrate the creation of one of the graphs.

- How does the graph help us answer the question 'Which can dimensions are best?'? [It identifies the minimum point and interprets the coordinates.]

Solution notes

The radius of the cylinder with minimum surface area is approximately 3.74 cm and its height is 7.50 cm (see resource sheet 8).

The filter and the funnel

Modelling and optimisation

Prerequisite knowledge
- Volume and surface area
- Pythagoras' theorem

Why do this unit?

This problem reinforces the use of a spreadsheet for optimisation problems, explores the relationship between volume and surface area, and considers extreme cases.

Time

Two lessons

Resources

A plastic funnel could be a useful visual aid
CD-ROM: spreadsheet, problem sheet, resource sheet
NRICH website (optional):
www.nrich.maths.org, January 2005, 'Fence it'; November 2007, 'Funnel'

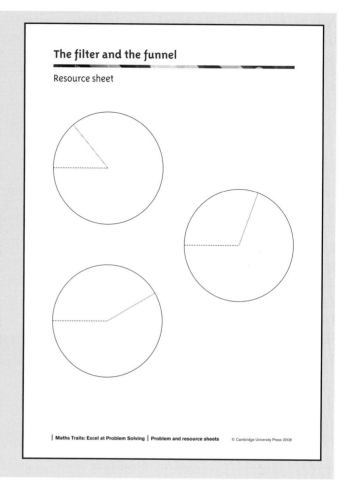

The filter and the funnel

Resource sheet

| Maths Trails: Excel at Problem Solving | Problem and resource sheets   © Cambridge University Press 2008

Introducing the unit

This problem is about maximising the volume of a cone.

Take a circle of diameter 10 cm, cut along a radius and show how a cone can be formed by passing one cut edge beneath the other, creating an overlap.

- As the overlap increases, the height of the cone increases. What happens to the volume? [It increases to start with and then decreases.]
- Estimate by eye when the maximum volume occurs.

The volume for a cone is one third the cylinder that it could just fit into ($\frac{1}{3}\pi r^2 h$). Measure the base radius and height for a cone made from any overlap and model calculating its volume with the pupils.

The resource sheet provides three circles with different overlaps marked. Pupils can make each of these cones (fastened with paper clips) and calculate their volumes.

- What fraction of overlap do you think would give the maximum cone volume? [using an overlap of about 60° from the original circle – the accuracy of pupils' answers will be refined later by using the spreadsheet]
- The original circle had a radius of 5 cm. If I want to make it into a cone with a base radius of 4 cm, what fraction of the circle must overlap? [One fifth must overlap. Because the radius is reducing in the ratio 5:4 the circumference must also reduce in the ratio 5:4 and so must the angle at the centre. $\frac{4}{5}$ is left so $\frac{1}{5}$ must be lost.]
- The original radius length (5 cm) has become the slope length of the cone. If the radius of the base is 4 cm can we calculate the height of that cone? [3 cm using Pythagoras' theorem]
- *Extension*: If we want to get a height of 4 cm, what overlap is needed? [Find the

radius (3 cm) using Pythagoras' theorem. The reduction ratio is 5:3 for the radius, the same for the circumference, and so the overlap must be $\frac{2}{5}$ of the original circle.]

This activity can be continued, calculating overlaps needed to create a cone with a specific radius or a specific height. This is intellectually demanding and should not be rushed; developing a good foundation of understanding ahead of the spreadsheet work is important.

Main part of the unit

From cut to cone

Show the group the sheet 'From cut to cone' on the spreadsheet and discuss the calculation in each column.

Choosing an angle of overlap determines the reduction in cone base circumference and therefore the base radius. Once the base radius is known, Pythagoras' theorem allows us to calculate the height. Using the height and the base radius, the volume can be calculated.

The maximum volume occurs with an overlap of about 66°. The graph provides a useful view of how the volume varies with overlap angle.

The funnel problem

Show the group the problem sheet and discuss how a funnel is based on a cone.

Discuss what might be meant by 'best shape'; a number of valid suggestions might be offered.

Draw in the commercial constraint of using a minimum amount of plastic. [The cone with the greatest volume for its surface area will be the 'best shape'.]

Examine the sheet 'Funnel' and discuss the stages of calculation with the group. Note that the height is determined for each radius if we have a fixed volume. At this stage it would therefore be helpful if a cone shape can be found that uses the minimum surface area to contain 1 litre (1000 cm^3).

Column A holds radius values. Column B calculates the height based on a volume of 1000 cm^3 for each radius. The most useful formula for a cone's surface area is $\pi r l$ (see the solution notes for an explanation), where l is the slope length. Column C calculates the slope length with that radius and height, before calculating the surface area in column D using that formula.

Pupils may wish to construct spreadsheets of their own or amend the spreadsheet 'Funnel'. Explain that they will be expected to explain and justify their findings in the plenary, so they need to think about how they will present their findings.

Plenary

Share well-executed and systematic approaches to the final problem and good justifications of any generalisations.

Solution notes

Note that the formula for the surface area of the cone is found by lying it flat to make the sector of a circle. The radius of the circle is the slope length of the cone and the fraction of the circle present is $2\pi r/2\pi l$ (or r/l as discovered earlier in the unit) – the circumference of the cone base compared

with the circumference of this circle of radius l. The area is therefore $\pi l^2 \times r/l = \pi r l$.

For a volume of 1000 cm^3 the radius which gives the minimum surface area is 8.77 cm and the height is 12.99 cm.

For the minimum surface area the ratio of the height to the radius will always be $\sqrt{2}$. It does not depend on the volume of the funnel.

Some Excel techniques explained

This section contains important Excel techniques. These are described in the units where they occur and are collected below for reference.

INT function

Remember in Excel '=' is needed at the start of a formula to be calculated; otherwise the program assumes that INT is just a word you want to type.

The INT function drops the decimal fraction part of a number and returns the integer part. For example, =INT(4.1623) would return 4 and =INT(4.8623) would also return 4. INT has many uses. Getting at the individual digits in a number is of particular value for problem solving.

If cell A1 contained the value 628 then the following formula would extract the hundreds digit: =INT(A1/100)

For the tens digit a similar but slightly more involved formula is needed:
=INT(A1/10) – 10*INT(A1/100)
This formula calculates the number of whole tens (62) and subtracts ten times the number of whole hundreds.

The formula to get just the units digit is
A1–10*INT(A1/10)
This is the complete number minus ten times the number of whole tens.

ABS function

The ABS function returns the absolute value. ABS(20–50) would return 30 not –30.

MOD function

The MOD (modulo) function returns the remainder when one value is divided by another. MOD(15,2) would return 1. MOD(15,3) would return 0.

The MOD function is particularly valuable when exploring factors, multiples and remainders.

Absolute cell references

The normal state for the cell references in a formula is to be a relative reference. This means that when a formula is copied into a new position, the new formula automatically has cell references that relate to the new position rather than maintaining the cell references used in the original formula. For example:

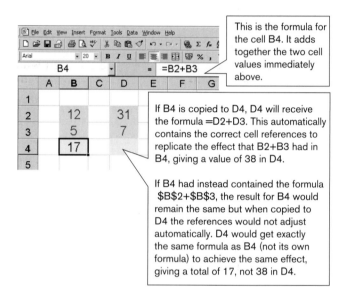

This is the formula for the cell B4. It adds together the two cell values immediately above.

If B4 is copied to D4, D4 will receive the formula =D2+D3. This automatically contains the correct cell references to replicate the effect that B2+B3 had in B4, giving a value of 38 in D4.

If B4 had instead contained the formula B2+B3, the result for B4 would remain the same but when copied to D4 the references would not adjust automatically. D4 would get exactly the same formula as B4 (not its own formula) to achieve the same effect, giving a total of 17, not 38 in D4.

Producing a table for a function of two independent variables

As an example here is a simple tables grid:

		2	3	5	7
3	6	9	15	21
4	8	12	20	28
7	14	21	35	49
9	18	27	45	63

- The cell C3 contains the formula: =C$2*$B3 (i.e. a product formed from two factors)
- The symbol * means multiply in Excel, and although the functions we need to investigate will often involve more than simple multiplication, the process explained below is easy enough to apply even when the function itself is complicated.
- In the illustration above, C2 is the factor from the top row and B3 is the factor from the left hand column.

- The dollar sign, $ in front of the 2 (C$2) and in front of the B ($B3) used in the C3 formula =C$2*$B3, ensures that when the formula is copied from C3 to any other cell the first factor will continue to be taken from row 2 and the second factor will always be taken from column B.

- Once the correct formula has been entered in C3, the keystrokes for the copy manoeuvre are:
  - Select C3 (just click on it).
  - Choose **Copy** from the **Edit** menu.
  - Highlight (click and drag) the C3:F6 range.
  - Choose **Paste** from the **Edit** menu.

- The formula from C3 is copied to all cells in the C3:F6 range. The formula is adjusted for each new position except where a $ sign was placed. As a result, all the new formulae will have a 2 in the first factor and a B in the second factor.

Producing a graph

Two units in this book use graphs. The values in cells give a feel for individual 'spot' values, but a graph can complement that by showing the overall shape of the function. The steps are straight-forward with a little practice.

- Select the two columns of values to plot against each other.
- If the columns are not adjacent, select the first and then hold down the control key while you drag to select the second column.
- From the **Insert** menu choose **Chart**
- Select XY (Scatter) and complete the dialogue box to get the graph.

Inserting an increment button (spinner) or scroll bar to control the values in a cell

Many spreadsheets included in this book use spinners when a value is to vary. Without these buttons the keyboard must be used for all changes to cell values. Sometimes it is desirable to keep attention on the spreadsheet and not to use the keyboard at all for entering or changing cell values (e.g. with an interactive whiteboard). This can be achieved using increment buttons. There are two types available. Excel calls them spinners and scroll bars.

The spinner is a two-part button made from an up arrow and a down arrow. The control is set

on the spinner so that the values stay within a chosen range and only change in steps of a specified size. The scroll bar is the same but with a slider between the two arrows.

Spinners and scroll bars are found on the Forms toolbar. To obtain this toolbar go to the **View** menu, choose toolbar and select the toolbar Forms. Drag the toolbar to the top or bottom of the workspace. It will then be located amongst the toolbar buttons already there.

Choose the tool (spinner or scroll bar) from the Forms toolbar and then click and drag out the rectangular outline for the button you wish to create. It can be any size. Note that the size and other characteristics can be changed at any time.

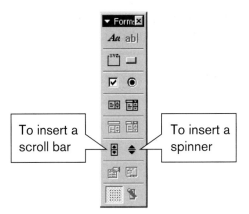

After you have a button on the workspace the next task is to connect it to a cell.

Right-click on the button, choose Format Control, and complete the dialogue box.

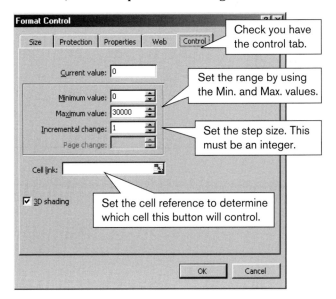

Conditional formatting

Suppose we want a cell that has numbers in blue to switch to numbers in red if that cell value becomes negative. Here's how that's done.

- Make sure that the correct cell is selected.
- From the **Format** menu choose **Conditional Formatting** and a dialogue box will appear.

- Set the condition Cell Value Is, less than, 0 as shown in the illustration.
- Click the Format button on the dialogue box to set the appearance that the cell is to have if the condition is met. Notice the limited range of format change that is possible. You can only set the font colour, the fill (background) colour and the cell border colour.
- Click **OK**, and then **OK** back on the Condition box.

Make the cell become negative, then positive, then 0, and so on, checking that the conditional formatting is triggered correctly.

You will notice that a lot more than negative cell values can be tested for.

There is an even more powerful possibility.

The first field in the dialogue box can be set to 'Formula Is' instead of 'Cell Value Is'. The second field then contains a formula, rather than a simple numerical value, and has to start with an equals sign because that is how Excel identifies what follows as a formula to evaluate. This formula is the condition being tested for.

So, in this case, if this was conditional formatting set on cell C9, if C13 was greater than C14 the chosen alternative formatting for C9 would be triggered.

You need to explore this kind of feature for yourself to see other possibilities. There can be up to three independent conditions being tested, which lets cells, for example in 'Multiples grid', have a wide range of colour change possibilities.